First published in 2008 by
Appletree Press Ltd
The Old Potato Station
14 Howard Street South
Belfast BT7 1AP

Tel: +44 (028) 90 24 30 74
Fax: +44 (028) 90 24 67 56
Email: reception@appletree.ie
Web: www.appletree.ie

Copyright © Appletree Press, 2008
Text © Barry Kennerk 2008
Illustration © Julianne Gallagher, 2008

All rights reserved. Printed in India. No part of this publication may be reproduced or transmitted, in any form or by any means, electronic or mechanical, photocopying, recording, or in any information and retrieval system, without permission in writing from the publisher.

The Railway House – Tales from an Irish Fireside

A catalogue record for this book is available from the British Library.

ISBN-13: 978 1 84758 089 4

Desk & Marketing Editor: Jean Brown
Copy-editing: Jim Black
Cover Design: Stuart Wilkinson
Production Manager: Paul McAvoy

9 8 7 6 5 4 3 2 1

AP3537

THE
RAILWAY HOUSE

Tales from an Irish Fireside

Barry Kennerk

Appletree Press

For my wife and daughters

Contents

	Acknowledgements	*6*
	Preface	*8*
Chapter 1	A Night Caller	10
Chapter 2	The Rambling House	15
Chapter 3	Below in White's	21
Chapter 4	Our Dog Jack	26
Chapter 5	One Five Minutes' T'inkin'	29
Chapter 6	Saturday Confession	34
Chapter 7	"Don't be Ugly" Says Oul' Jack Ugan	40
Chapter 8	The Convent School	44
Chapter 9	On to the High School	49
Chapter 10	"Oh Jaysus, Have You a Ma?"	54
Chapter 11	Visitors to the House	59
Chapter 12	The Buttermilk and the Hat	67
Chapter 13	Tyre tracks on the Bog Road	73
Chapter 14	Trip to the Well	79
Chapter 15	Holidays in Dublin	83
Chapter 16	Autumn Divilment	92
Chapter 17	Going for the Cows	98
Chapter 18	Digging Turf	104
Chapter 19	Christmas Time	110
Chapter 20	Hunting the Wren	127
Chapter 21	The Dublin Jackeen	129
Chapter 22	Father Troy	134
Chapter 23	Stations of the Cross	138
Chapter 24	Kilmucklin	142
Chapter 25	Oul' Jackeen Feehan	149
Chapter 26	A Fireman's Girl	154
Chapter 27	The Humours of Kilkenny	157
Chapter 28	The Abbey Players	165
Chapter 29	Jam at Galls	171
Chapter 30	The Cards are Dealt (1943)	176
Chapter 31	Visit to Kilminchy	185
Chapter 32	Night before the Wedding	191
Chapter 33	Bringing Bread to Make Peace	197
	Epilogue	*200*

ACKNOWLEDGEMENTS

First and foremost, I would like to thank my Secondary School English teacher, Denise O'Brien.

Thereafter, there are many to whom I am indebted. My grandmother notwithstanding, among those who have aided me in my research are Eamonn Kelly, Seanchai (RIP), the Gaynor families in Tullamore, Carlow and London, the Finlay and Cregg families from Tullamore and the Holmes family, Ashfield, Clara. In particular, I would like to thank Mary Jane Gaynor for the time she took to patiently respond to all of my letters. To Noel Kelly, who took the time to meet me – my thanks.

Ellen Watt (née Gaynor) generously wrote from California on several occasions, and I would also like to thank her daughter Kathy Cross.

I have also received assistance from John Holmes of the Offaly Historical and Archaeological Society, to whom I am indebted. The other archives that I consulted were the aforementioned Railway Records Society (thanks to Brendan Pender), The Agricultural Museum, Co. Wexford and Premises Department CIE.

I would like to sincerely thank Nora Kavanagh, the principal of Scoil Bhríde, Clara, for helping me to obtain information from the school roll-book of 1923. She also went out of her way to provide details from the confirmation register and on the layout of the school building for the period during which my grandmother was a pupil there.

Of special mention are Catch Byrne, Haltkeeper at Clara Station and Billy Parkinson who so kindly gave up their time to help with retracing my great-grandfather's footsteps on the Tullamore–

Acknowledgements

Clara line. The assistance of retired railwayman Sean Maloney was also much appreciated.

Lest I forget, I would also like to thank the Kenny family of Clara for their excellent insight into fishing practices of the 1940s and Julianne Gallagher for her illustrations.

I would also like to thank local Portlaoise historians Mary Lawlor and John O'Brien for their assistance and for putting me in touch with Arthur Whelan, whose recollections of the Houlihan family home were invaluable.

I would like to thank all those who proofread the manuscript in its final stages and for their helpful suggestions and advice.

Lastly, but by no means least, I would like to thank the staff of Appletree Press for their interest and enthusiasm in the project.

I hope that the finished result will be reward enough for their assistance.

Barry Kennerk

PREFACE

The Railway House sits near an embankment at the end of a short boreen cutting through the esker ridge of the Ballinough Hills, Co. Offaly. Looking out past a level crossing onto the lonely expanse of Doury bog, it cuts a solitary presence in the surrounding landscape. On either end, its gable walls face towards the towns of Tullamore and Clara.

It was into this four-roomed home that my maternal grandmother, Kathleen Mary Gaynor, was born on 8th April 1914. Yellow-brown wallflowers rambled around the door and the little garden outside the house was filled with sweetpea. During the summer, the smell of creosote-coated sleepers filled the yard and there was the ever-present sight and sound of steam trains as drivers stopped their engines outside the hall door.

There had been Gaynors at Ashfield Crossing since House 224 was built, but my grandmother's was the third and last generation. During the latter part of the nineteenth century, her grandfather Joseph Gaynor had been employed by the Great Southern and Western Railway (GS&WR) as a 'Checker' – a position that entitled him and his family to rent-free occupation of the house. Later he had a family of six boys and two girls, and all of his sons worked in the same railway gang. In later adult life, most of these drifted away and took up positions elsewhere.

Tom was the only son who remained. In 1891, he had been given a six-month trial with his brothers' gang at a weekly rate of fourteen shillings and sixpence – a good wage considering that a factory worker only earned about ten shillings.

When his father retired in November 1897, he travelled to Kingsbridge Station (now Dublin Heuston Station) to take ownership of the railway house. The surviving GS&WR document displays his very shaky signature, recorded in the presence of Inspector Brackham. Whether this was as a result of nerves or the cold, we will never know.

Some years later, he was promoted to the position of Platelayer Ganger and was responsible for the twelve men who worked the section of track between mileposts 61¾ and 65¾. His yearly wages are recorded, as are the names of the various inspectors with whom he worked.

Unfortunately however, that is where the written records end. Whilst Irish railway records are replete with technical and financial details, they are poor on information concerning the inhabitants of the two and a half thousand CIE (Córas Iompair Éireann, the Irish transport company) properties still standing. In addition, a notable lack of recorded oral evidence has hampered efforts to research the lives of these men and their families. As a result, my grandmother's personal testimony fills an important and irreplaceable gap in our understanding.

If one abides by the notion that a book should not be written unless it has something meaningful to say, then this book will have been more than worthwhile. It is an attempt to open an insight into a life on the railway that has largely gone unwritten.

CHAPTER ONE

A Night Caller

The scream of the whistle comes over the noise of the train, and Ashfield crossing flashes past. Through the drifting steam we catch a glimpse of Clara down distant signal, fixed at Caution, and the whistle sounds again as the train enters the curve leading to the cutting which here divides the esker ridge.
J.P. O'Dea, 'Clara to Banagher' (II),
Journal of the Irish Railway Record Society No. 63: Feb 1974

The second rap on the railway house door woke my father from a deep sleep, and he sat drowsily on the edge of his bed for a moment before rising. Threatening violence to whomever might be outside, he was about to fumble for the lamp on the kitchen window-sill when he noticed a pale glimmer of light under the door jamb.

"Are you there, Mr Gaynor?" cried a muffled voice from the other side.

Lifting the latch, he peered straight into the lamp-lit features of a lad from Clara Station. He had cycled all the way down the line in the dark.

"A goods train…is after de-coupling…" he panted, pointing back towards the Station.

Following his hand, my father glanced in the direction of the railway hut. There, in the dark, a row of goods wagons creaked slowly to a standstill, coming to rest near the whistling board.

He sighed in annoyance. This was a regular occurrence on the Clara line. Approaching the station, drivers had to judge their speed properly so that if the engine was coming down a hill, they could keep the chains coupling the wagons taut. On this particular night, the 'India Special' with 80 wagons bound for the jute factory had rolled down the hill at Ashfield crossing at such speed that the wagons had crashed together. As they came up the incline, the buffers separated and a chain link had snapped.

The driver, unaware that part of his train was now missing, continued on to Clara. At the station, the absence of a signalling lamp on the last wagon alerted the haltkeeper to the problem, and he despatched a lad to the level crossing. Soon, the driver would reverse down the line to retrieve his missing wagons, having first waited a few minutes to allow them to coast to a stop.

"Wait here," my father instructed the railwayman, "until I get my gear together."

Returning to the bedroom, the springs creaked heavily as he sat on the edge of the bed and yanked his stockings on.

"Is everything all right?" my mother asked.

"Well that's a bugger," he sighed. "An oul' goods is after separating."

He pulled his boots on and not bothering to tie the laces, slipped out the back door. Unlike some other gatekeepers' cottages, there were no signals placed at our house, so he went to the shed to find his lantern, a red flag and some detonators.

The shed was made from railway sleepers standing upright, some of which still had their bolts attached. The other outbuildings housed the pony and the turf clamp, and a sickly sweet smell of creosote hung in the warm air.

When my father located the lantern in the dark, he lit the wick and brushed a moth away from the thick, oily glass. Then he wrapped the detonators inside the red flag, plodded around to the front of the house and issued instructions to the waiting railwayman.

"G'off down the line and set them detonators," he advised, carefully handing the charges to the young man. "You may set them ten yards apart."

"Begod and I will, Mr Gaynor," the milesman nodded. Yawning, my father watched as the lantern disappeared into the dark, swinging towards Tullamore.

Meanwhile, he began to rig up his own lamp. It fitted into a kind of bucket-shaped housing which when turned one way, showed green and indicated that the way was clear. On the other side, there was a red filter for 'danger' so he turned it to face that way.

The detonators were set as a precaution. There was a danger that the Tullamore stationmaster, believing that the line was clear, would hand the staff to an oncoming driver and allow the train to proceed. To prevent an accident, the loud bang of the detonators as they exploded under the train's wheels would alert the driver to the fact that all was not well. If this failed, my father would be standing at the railway crossing with the lantern by his side.

Meanwhile, he looked at his pocket watch. In the red glow from the lamp, he could see that it was an unreasonable hour to be abroad.

"Even the last oul' drunk from White's must be tucked into bed long 'go," he mused wanly. Soon, my mother, feeling the empty space in the bed beside her would be sure to stir.

In sleep, she had murmured Johnny's name. That day, it had been ten years since the visiting priest confirmed Communion for their bedridden child. His brother Larry (God rest him) also had a little one buried above in St John's in Kilkenny.

Then a faint tingling sound reminded him that his wife's goat, restrained by its tether, had moved somewhere further along the embankment, and as clear as an altar bell, he also recalled the memory of their dead son.

But the evening was quiet otherwise, except for the indignant *crawk* of a red grouse disturbed from sleep out on Doury Bog. As he waited, the cool breeze blowing across the turf banks came as a welcome relief from the dull summer warmth of the kitchen.

After what seemed like an age, the faint sound of an engine reversing bolstered my father's flagging spirits and he moved into action. Jogging briskly along the stony embankment, he passed the railway hut and stopped just past the whistling board. Waving his lamp slowly from side to side, he indicated to the approaching driver and fireman that they had almost reached their errant wagons.

The hissing arc from his lantern was drowned as the train approached – wagons first – in a blaze of light and steam. As the engine passed, a soot-bedecked fireman wearing a pilot coat poked his head around the footplate. As his eyes fell across my father, a Moorish smile broke over his grimy features.

"Hould on there mister, till we dandle on up to these wagons," he shouted good-naturedly. His Dublin brogue carried clear on the night air.

Beside the fireman, my father could make out the white-gloved form of the driver who was busy shutting off the regulator and applying the steam brake to bring his engine to a full stop.

Once the train had halted, the fireman jumped down and pumped my father's hand vigorously.

"We made a terrible bad job of that run," he laughed.

My father looked at the young man with bemusement.

"Had ye a hard watch?" he asked.

"Jaysus we did," the Dublin man replied in earnest, casting a dispirited look towards the prone figure of the driver on the footplate. "Father Byrne doesn't talk to no one when he's driving – says he didn't come this far to hear me mouthing out of me."

As the fireman slipped easily along the embankment, my father mused to himself. A young chap like that on the Athlone run, probably out of a Dublin tenement somewhere – only just made fireman. 'Ah, a fella only gets consolation at the end of a bottle,' a driver had said to him once in White's. Well, he could at least understand where the sentiment lay. A man such as my father had cause to feel lucky. He had fresh air, fresh vegetables and a free roof over his head. So while the immaculately dressed driver began to bark orders to his unfortunate fireman, he strolled open-laced; content – but not a little reflective – whistling back down the line to bed.

CHAPTER TWO

The Rambling House

In a rambling house, ten o'clock was the usual time for everyone to go home, signalled by my mother's announcement to everyone around the hearth that the fifteen decades of the Rosary was about to start. Well you never saw anything like the almighty rush to get out the door. They may as well have been told that the house was on fire, because once the door was locked, they would have no choice but to say all the decades.

While the prayers were in progress, my brother Larry usually waited outside. He planned his entrance perfectly so that by the time he lifted the latch, the Rosary would be almost over. Then, with an air of piety he would come in, pull over a chair and sit facing the back of it to recite what we called the 'trimmings'. These were prayers for the holy 'sowels' as the old people called them and for people who died without anyone to pray for them. He got off lightly.

One evening, when the Rosary was over and the ramblers had gone, my mother took the iron out from under the table with a sense of relief and opened the box of Robin starch powder with its picture of the little bird on the front. With one stout hand, she poured some of the powder into an empty enamel basin and left it ready for the hot water. She was a big, fat woman with small round-framed glasses, and she wore her hair in a bun which was never down, except in the morning time when she was getting dressed. Her long dress, which she wore under a double-pocketed *praiscín* (apron), helped to protect her feet and ankles from immodesty.

Earlier that evening, the shirts had been scrubbed on a washboard. As my mother starched them, I went to fetch the ball of blue. That consisted of a small soapy ball inside a muslin bag and when I squeezed it into the basin; the water became cloudy. It was guaranteed to have the shirts gleaming white.

When they were almost dry and stiff as pokers, I began to prepare them for ironing. The box iron, made by Pierce's of Wexford, had a latch in its back into which I placed a lump of iron stamped with a number '3', the same shape and size as the box. The purpose of the box was to keep the clothes clean, since the iron piece was always red hot and dusty when it came out of the grate.

After I had been ironing for a few minutes, I noticed that the first lump of iron was growing cold. Removing it with a piece of cloth, I set it down near the table and lifted the second one off the hearth with the long tongs. I waited until my mother had opened the clasp of the box and nimbly placed it inside. Then I took up the iron and continued where I had left off. Despite being so awkward, it was the best method that we had.

We looked forward to a cup of tea and to the treacle cake that we had hidden that day from the lads. As I looked in at them in the settle bed, I thought about how hard we had worked to ensure that they would look their best at Sunday Mass.

The house was quiet; apart from the sound of the kettle on the crane, the dull thud of the iron and the occasional sound of a lone corncrake on nearby Dourly Bog.

When the three shirts had been hung on the backs of the chairs, I took the heavy iron kettle from its resting-place over the hearth. In those days, we always left the tea bubbling away because water took a long time to boil. As I filled her cup, my mother glanced at me sternly.

"I hope you bolted that door," she chided.

Raising my eyes to heaven, I set the kettle down.

"Of *course* I did," I replied, knowing damn well that I was only half sure. You see, in those days there were often farmers' workmen abroad at night, and many of them rambled home past our house. My mother was always afraid that one of them might get in because they had a tendency to stay all night if they were let.

No sooner were the words out of my mouth than I heard the little iron gate creaking open.

"I told you to bolt that door!" my mother cried, but there was no time to argue. In a panic, I fired the kettle down and made for the bedroom. My mother had just enough time to attend to the paraffin lamp before she found a hiding place. Our light consisted of a big round globe standing on a brass fitting. Lifting it abruptly off the sill, she fumbled for the wick and turned it down low, to make whoever was outside think there was no one in.

As I stood behind the door, I could hear the heavy step of a man coming up the path, past the little wooden paling that bordered the sweetpea-scented garden. Then the sound stopped and for a moment I expected the owner of the feet to see no light and go back the way he had come.

Outside, the level crossing was quiet and since the evening train had passed some time ago, the silence was unrelieved. In my mind's eye, I could see the whitewashed walls of the house gleaming faintly, picking out the edge of the green-painted front door and its metal '225'. Underneath a vine – bare of its orange-brown wallflowers – some stranger would be standing. I thought of my father who was drinking in the town, but he was not due back for at least another hour.

Suddenly, my heart jumped! The latch lifted and the door creaked open. It swung drunkenly on its frame for a few minutes while we waited anxiously for whomever it was to show themselves.

Then, without further ado, an old workman staggered into the wallpapered kitchen. Furrowing his work-lined face in the dim lamplight, he paused to take a look around.

On the kitchen table was evidence of a hasty departure – two full mugs of tea, an uncut treacle cake and some freshly ironed shirts hanging on the backs of the chairs. Beyond that, the lads lay sleeping in their settle bed. It folded up as a seat during the day but with the addition of a straw mattress, it could be taken out for them to sleep in at night. It was an awful frosty night, and the open door carried a breeze that made the tiny red paraffin lamp sputter under the Sacred Heart picture.

Through the crack in the bedroom door, we could make out the man's dusty trousers and worn boots. I gasped as he lurched over to the settle bed, thinking to myself that he could have taken out a knife and killed the lads as they slept. Instead, he looked down at my eldest brother who lay at the edge of the bed and his face broke into a gommish (gnome-like) smile.

I had nicknamed Tommie 'The Boar' because he could go for you bald-headed. For similar reasons, Ned was named 'The Weasel' and then there was Larry, who shared the same nickname as a ragged workman called 'Fliggit'.

"God, boys," the visitor said, suddenly reminded of the cold shed he slept in. "Do ye know it's a cauld night outside?"

Then, wide-eyed from this sudden revelation, he staggered around the settle bed and looked in at them from the other side. The three of them were dead to the world.

"Boys, it's very cauld," he persisted, rubbing his hands and thinking that he would have loved to be in there beside them. "That's a grand place to be in, boys oh boys!"

Meanwhile, we could do nothing but watch whilst the workman staggered this way and that around the snoring boys, never minding their sleepy murmurs about skittles and cards.

Eventually, to our great relief, he toddled out of the door as quietly as a lamb and a few moments later, we heard him climbing noisily over the stile. As she turned the lamp wick back up, my mother said with annoyance, "Didn't I tell you to lock that door?"

I gave her an anxious look but then the two of us took a fit of laughing at the good of it.

But despite the precautions that she took with the lamp, my mother was not a woman who shied away from company. At a respectable hour, it was quite usual for one rambler to be going out of the front door as another was coming in by the back. But once all the card games were over, she kept a watchful eye over who was coming down the lane. From time to time, we used to hear an old soldier mumbling to himself as he walked past the gate. The man was suffering from shellshock, a condition caused by long months spent in the trenches of France, but he was harmless compared to some of the other characters who roamed abroad at night, because my mother might never be shut of them.

In particular, she was always prepared for the workman's employer, Johnny Wogan, who was worse than his employee for drink and often came past after spending the day in White's. Johnny had a pony and sidecart but although he trusted the animal to know its own road, most nights he was barely able to stay sitting long enough to come down to the crossing gates. My mother always made sure to lock the door so that he never got in, because once there he might stay half the evening.

One night, as we sat around the dying embers of the fire, we heard Johnny coming down the lane with a feed of porter inside him as usual. In a panic, my mother ran to lock the door and put out the light so he would think there was no one in. The clip-clop of hooves continued until the pony reached the crossing gates and then they stopped. Unfortunately, the sudden halt roused Johnny out of his stupor, so he stumbled off the car and made straight for our hall door.

At the same moment, Mike Doorley, who was a regular in our house, struck a match against the stone floor to light his pipe. Clay pipes or 'dudeens' were the norm among country people, who would pull away at them and blind you with the smoke. In a panic, my mother gave the pipe a clout because she thought Johnny would see the light of the match, but in her haste broke it into a hundred bits on the stone flag.

"Jaysus, me pipe!" cried Mike in surprise.

Johnny came up to the door singing 'Nora' but got fed up after a few minutes and 'Nora'd' off with himself. As we waited, it seemed as though as though he had only gone as far as the little gate when he changed his mind and decided to sing another verse:

> *The golden-dewed daffodils shone, Nora,*
> *And danced in the breeze on the lea,*
> *When I first said, I loved only you, Nora,*
> *And you said, you loved only me.*

Lord, sure he hadn't an ounce. He stumbled over the words: '*And you…you said…you only loved me*'.

"Well I'll answer that fella," cried Mike Doorley, "with a bucket of water if you let me out at him."

"You will not," laughed my poor mother.

CHAPTER THREE

Below in White's

Relaxing in the smoky company of the drivers, my father fished in his waistcoat pocket for the bowl of his pipe. On benches either side of him sat two train drivers – 'The Knacker' O'Keeffe and 'Slasher' Walsh. When Walsh stopped his engine outside our hall door, we knew he was sure to have a couple of drinks in the kitchen with my father and run his engine faster to make up for lost time. Together with the Knacker, he had come into town with a goods train and was staying overnight at Clara junction before carrying on the next morning to Athlone.

Bearing down on them with a full pint of stout was their good friend Mike Doorley. Mike lived on our laneway with his wife Hanoria, and they had a small pony called 'Ciss'. It was a weekday and, as usual, the men could be found drinking below in Michael Henry White's. Many of the railwaymen spent time away from their families and took lodgings overnight in towns up and down the line. As a result, they got to know each other very well and most could buy and sell my father.

"Tell the lads what happened again over the bikes," Mike prompted, taking a large mouthful from his glass. Eyes wide and upper lip festooned with a moustache of froth, he waited for my father's pipe to light.

"Well," the ganger started, between exploratory puffs, "it was all a matter of L. s. & d."

Leaning closer towards the men, he took a closeted glance in the direction of the bar.

"Do ye remember the young barman who used to work here? Well didn't I decide to go guarantor with him on a bicycle. Had me heart broken over it – always asking was I going to put my name to it. Anyway, to make a long story short, a while afterwards, a letter arrives out to Ashfield saying that your man has defaulted on his payments and that I'm liable for the whole bledy lot."

The men shook their heads and muttered amongst themselves. A line had been crossed amongst them, but they wanted to hear more before making up their minds about the erstwhile barman.

"So anyhow, I asked around below at the station and didn't I find that your man had given up the job and was gone altogether. Now I was rightly sunk, so I had to go over to Moate to find his priest of a brother."

My father took a long draught from his pint before continuing.

"The next thing was, I arrived at the priest's house, and into the kitchen. 'Now,' says the priest, 'You should be ashamed of yourself, a married man with children, going guarantor for the likes of him, when it's food you should be putting on the table.' Then without another word, he takes me down to t'oul' shed at the back of the house and shows me six brand new bikes, none of them ped for. The barman ownded the whole lot."

The men agreed unanimously that an unwritten rule of principle had been broken and the Knacker O'Keeffe spoke bravely about what he would do if he came across the barman in Moate or elsewhere.

Suddenly short taken, my father stretched out one leg, allowing him to manoeuvre his watch out of a waistcoat pocket. Once the chain had been fished out, he felt the hard bulk of the watch-dial in his hand.

Seeing that there was still plenty of time, he stood up, scuffing away the sawdust at his feet. Leaving the bench, he passed the bar where men like him tossed their ninepence across the counter, bought pints and chewed tobacco which they deposited noisily into brass spittoons. Two barmen served both the bar and the grocery counter at the other end. When customers came in for their weekly shopping, one of the lads would go out to attend them and return to serve bottles of porter or a glass of whiskey.

At the back of the pub, my father came across a familiar face – that of a workman called Joe Casey, who often stopped at our house for a glass of buttermilk. In the process of making his ablutions, he turned animatedly.

"Do you know what 'tis Mr Gaynor?" he said. "When I make me water on a windy day; 'tis the only t'ing in life that ever comes back to me!"

My father grinned. It wasn't just railwaymen who patronised the pubs in the town. A lot of the men working for local farmers also drank in White's and many of them spent their entire week's wages on beer.

Later that evening, Larry was sent to fetch my father home. My mother, anxious over the recent death of the Tailor Spollen, often tried to dissuade him from cycling if she could manage it. Her husband would not however be discouraged from drinking and 'driving'.

"I'm well able to make me own way," he told his youngest son. "I'm well fed with porter, but by God I can make me own way."

He rose heavily from his seat and felt his pockets to ensure that all was intact. Following Mike Doorley, he made for the door, whistling aimlessly to himself 'Oh Whiskey, You're the Divil, You're Driving me Astray.'

As he came out onto Main Street, he noticed a street musician playing a melodeon. Now, besides drinking, the other great love that my father had in life was music. The player, who was hoping to catch some of the passing trade when the pubs closed, was sitting near the cobbled gutter with his back to the roadway. As was the custom in those days, he had a hat at his feet. My father, who was so full of life, heard the music and got out in the middle of the dusty road to dance a hornpipe. A crowd gathered round to listen when he burst into song:

> *Whiskey, ye're the divil, ye're leadin' me astray*
> *Over hills and mountains and to Americae*
> *You're sweeter, stronger, decenter, you're spunkier than tae*
> *O whiskey, you're my darlin' drunk or sober.*

When he had finished entertaining, he leant, doubled up in laughter against the telegraph pole at the other side of Main Street. The crowd of men dispersed homeward then and were lost beyond the circle of pub-light – no streetlight after ten o'clock since Goodbodys paid for the gas in the lamps.

After a few moments, he staggered back to where Larry stood waiting with the bikes.

"Tom, do you remember the night of the big wind?" Mike said, elbowing him playfully.

"Would that be tonight Mike, do ye think?" my father answered, stifling a belch.

The question was something that the Government used to ask old people years ago to find out their age for granting the pension, but Mike had that as a sort of cant.

After a while, the two men and boy picked up their bikes leaning along the wall outside and cycled down the dark main street of Clara, passing the wooden-shuttered shops on the way. Then they took a wide turn at D.E. Williams and swung left down River Street, scarcely looking right to see whether there was anything coming from Bridge Street; on under the railway bridge and out by the main road.

In those days, it was an established fact that a man, once drunk, could not freewheel on a bike. Whether going up or coming down a hill, he was sure to pedal like the hammers of hell and that's what happened to the tailor – our uncle from Daingean and a relation on my father's side. He was peddling down a hill well jarred when he hit a stone and came off his bike. A neighbour drove his trap into Church Street for help but when Doctor O'Hara reached the spot, the tailor was dead.

"Ah Pat," he sighed. "You finished yourself at last."

After a couple of miles, my father and Mike – not having had the tailor's misfortune – made the turn for Ashfield down a dusty boreen. Mike waved goodnight when they reached the big beech tree at the top of the lane, leaving the two Gaynors to cycle on. Hell for leather, they rattled perilously down the hill 'over hills and mountains and to Americae!'

When, at an unholy hour, the sound of bicycles announced their return, my mother threw her eyes up to heaven and muttered, "Jesus, he'll come in now after a few drinks and start training the dog."

CHAPTER FOUR

Our Dog Jack

My father had Jack trained to jump hoops and to smoke a crooked pipe. Night after night, he stood in the middle of the floor and the dog – knowing what his master was at – would sit up waiting to jump. Once Jack had jumped, he would shift the hoop. By degrees, he could get the dog to do the whole kitchen in a circle.

My father went very hard on Jack and used to beat the lard out of him to make him sit up, not minding the fact that the dog might be dying with the hunger. Eventually he got it and when I was eating at the table I often looked down to see him on his tail with his little paws out, begging for a crust of bread. In the end, the dog did nearly everything but talk.

It was just as well because our last dog had not been so obedient. When he started to worry sheep, people on the lane began to get anxious about being bitten. There was a great superstition amongst the older people that if they were bitten by a dog, their fate would become tied to that of the animal. From that day on, whatever happened to the dog was sure to happen to them.

One evening, a local farmer came down to the railway house in a murderous temper. Standing with his arms folded, he argued his case with my father.

"I'm not leaving until you do away with that dog," he shouted.

Forcing his hand on the matter, the farmer was not satisfied until my father fetched a dusty jute sack from the shed and put the little animal into it.

"Now," he quipped as the Jack Russell yelped inside the bag, "he'll kill no more sheep."

Under cover of darkness, the two men made their way up the lane towards the Brosna River. They hardly spoke to each other as they walked, but when they reached the riverbank, the farmer said he was satisfied and left my father to carry out the deed on his own.

Another dog had a tendency to chase trains. Afraid that he would get hurt, my father was determined to frighten him out of the habit. In those days, drivers used to vent steam from both sides when they were bringing down the boiler pressure. In his wisdom, my father thought that if the driver let out steam passing the house, the dog would jump with the fright. On the designated day, the train rounded the bend and blew a shrill toot as it passed the whistling board near the hut.

As it passed the house, my father couldn't see his hand in front of him for the steam, but when it cleared he was dismayed to find that instead of jumping away from the track, the poor dog had gone under the wheels of the train.

When Jack showed signs of misbehaving, a softer approach was needed. As my father set off for work one morning, he whistled to the dog to come to heel, and cycled the few miles into Clara station with him. When a passenger train came in, he asked the guard to take the dog with him in the van to Athlone and let him out there so that he might be done with him. Jack never knew a thing and was horsed in among parcels and God knows what. Then the train pulled out and, as far as everyone was concerned, that was that.

The next day however, Larry was playing around the railings outside. As he knelt down to pick something up, he felt two little paws on his back. The little dog had run all the way from Athlone – about 17 miles or so – to find his way home! We couldn't get rid of him then and when my father heard what had happened, we had to keep him.

Soon afterwards, I set out with Jack for Egan's shop which was on the Tullamore Road. In those days, the countryside was full of huxtery shops that sold occasional items such as bread, tea, butter and milk. Although many of these shops were just temporary affairs set up in farmyards and parlour rooms, they saved people from the bother of going into town. I often sat in between Paddy and Nanny Egan with a cut of bread and jam and forgot to come home.

I had taken the little dog with me in my arms because he was a divil for birds and I worried that he might jump into a hedge. As we neared the shop however, Jack's little scut tail began to go like mad and he started to bark.

Without warning, he sprung out of my arms right into the path of an oncoming bread van on the main road. The driver, realising that he had hit something, skidded to a halt and ran back to where I stood. When he saw me crying, he told me to leave the dog and let him die there on the side of the road.

"He won't d-d-die anywhere," I sobbed. "I'm b-bringing him home."

I put him under my arms and roared the whole way home, with the dog roaring as well.

CHAPTER FIVE

One Five Minutes' T'inkin'

One cold morning, when Joe Burke arrived late for work, my father had good cause to look at his pocket watch. The whole gang were hard at work 'centre shoring' – a job that involved digging out stones from underneath the sleepers for drainage, but Joe just stood watching.

As he stood on the embankment, his shadow fell across the animated shape of my father, who, up until that moment had been working hard.

"God damn it," he shouted, suddenly noticing the presence of his errant milesman. He stood up and looked at his watch. "Are you only coming now?" he puffed, wiping his brow with a grimy hand. "Sure you're mad late. You'll get me sacked!"

He was always on his guard for bad time keeping, especially since he had been forced the previous year to sack a man called Paddy Lyons for it. But unfazed in the slightest by this reaction, Joe rambled on.

"Ah, do you know what 'tis Mr Gaynor," he replied, "I was just t'inkin' walking along there now."

"Ah, thinking me arse," my father muttered.

But Joe kept on, "I was just t'inkin'. D'ya know sometimes one five minutes' t'inkin' is better than a day's work?"

That same morning, a man carrying a flag walked slowly down the frosty line towards Clara station. Three-quarters of a mile behind him rolled a bogie laden with tools for my father's gang. The bogie was a flat open car, moved by hand, and when it reached the wooden bridge where the milesmen waited, the 'driver' jammed a shovel against the front wheel, bringing the vehicle to a halt.

Waiting for the tools stood a motley assortment of men, most of whom wore cloth caps and homespun kneecaps made from straw. One or two carried tool belts clipped at the waist and held in place by a strong pair of braces. Immediately, my father set about equipping them with shovels.

They were joined by Mattie Burke, who lived at house 224 near Clara Station. He carried a two-stone fang wrench on his shoulder and as he walked, he shifted the weight from shoulder to shoulder. On this particular morning, he was lucky. Some of the men had carried the same weight for four miles.

When he arrived, Mattie greeted the men and took stock of the line underfoot.

"Begod Mr Gaynor," he exclaimed, tapping an old cast-off chair with the edge of his wrench. "This must date back to the year you become a ganger."

"The year after," my father mused, staring at the iron piece at Mattie's foot. The chair, dated 1908, read WP&CO. MG&WR was stamped proudly on its reverse side. Then, breaking from his thoughtful stare, he cracked his fingers briskly. "Sure we'll need a few chairs to hould this rail in place," he said.

A young milesman called John Keaney was standing nearby.

"Why would you need that oul' yoke?" he questioned.

Mattie cast a disapproving glance in John's direction, but my father just grinned broadly.

"Ah now Mattie," he laughed, "the lad has to start somewhere."

The reproached Mattie looked downward and stubbed the rail sullenly with his foot. Ignoring him, my father continued for the young man's benefit.

"We have to replace a faulty bull-head rail," he explained. "It doesn't have a base, so we may hould it in place at each sleeper, and your iron bracket is called a chair."

He stooped down and lifted an iron piece at Mattie's foot. Taking its weight in his hands, he went on: "You see, this chair foots the rail – it could weigh about four stone. Take a hoult of it and see for yourself," he gestured, offering it to the young linesman.

"T'oul' chairs are grouped into a poundage scale," Mattie suddenly chimed in. "An 'A' chair is 87lb whereas a 'B' chair could be between 90 to 95lb in weight. You need the grades, depending on how much weight the line is expected to take at different points along its length."

"Begod Mattie," my father said in amazement. "That you may go to heaven in a kettle!"

Soon, the men were paired with the gang who worked the station yard. My father's men were responsible for general maintenance between mileposts 61¾ and 65¾. A granite 64¾ milepost stood near the yardman's patch but although my father's territory was a mile past that on the Athlone side, he upheld the general rule that the wooden bridge was the dividing line where his milesmen gave way to the shunting and pulling of wagons.

Mindful of this, he sent one man from each gang to inform the signalman. Even if the gang was working four miles from the cabin, somebody would have to walk or cycle to let the signalman know in case a train might be due.

While they waited, the rest of the men stood on the embankment, rubbing their hands to keep out the chill. It was so cold that during the morning, the station gang had wrapped the station's water hose in *sugán* – a kind of hay rope – to stop it from freezing. So far, the remedy seemed to have worked and trains were taking on water with little difficulty. Having been through the 'big snow' some winters before, it paid to be prepared for winter weather.

Meanwhile, the signalman in charge, hearing about the work that was due on the line, kept his signals at danger. One of the milesmen then stayed at the signal box, put down three detonators and took out his hand danger signals. The second milesman set out back towards my father to let him know that all was in place.

When he returned, the rest of the gang set to work.

"Ye may use the hommer," my father instructed.

The frosty weather was ideal, since under such conditions, two or three taps on each side of the triangle-shaped fangbolt was enough to cause it to fracture and break. It could then be freed easily from the timber it gripped. When the men were ready to lift, my father – ever the boss – moved down the line, marshalling them as if they were on parade.

"Ye lads move over there," he ushered. "That'll l'ave three o' ye on each side for hoistin' the rail."

When he was satisfied, he looked at his watch and gave the order. Then, working together, the six milesmen, each carrying a special type of tongs, lifted the rail off the track with a 'haaaaaaaay up!' With a heavy thud, they dropped it at the edge of the embankment, away from the path of oncoming trains.

Next, the new rail was carefully lowered into position. To save them from stooping constantly, the milesmen put a long attachment onto the handle of the wrench so that they could tighten the fang-bolts from a standing position. As they worked, my father occasionally let out a shout to Jack Moylan or one of the other men: "You're not tightening that bolt enough. Give it another half turn."

The keys, when knocked into the chairs were driven by the men in the direction in which the trains would run. The chairs themselves held the rail tilted slightly out of the vertical in their jaws. The tilt, which was one in twenty, held the centre-line of the rail exactly at right-angles to the face of the wheel-tyre, which was coned; and it also ensured that the rail would be safely in position even if every key along the length was knocked out. There was more to track-laying than met the eye.

When the job was finished, my father rubbed his jaw thoughtfully and looked at the line from all angles. It was a good piece of work. Nevertheless, he knew that several weeks might pass before the track had settled properly or 'lined up', so he asked Mattie, who lived nearest the repair, to keep an eye on it and to make adjustments where necessary.

In the months and years afterwards, this section of line was checked regularly because it got the heaviest use. Sometimes, the milesman would find a worn-down chair or sole plate and when this happened, a flat piece of iron known as a 'shim' was placed underneath it. This process of raising or lowering the iron components of the line was called 'shimming', and it helped to keep everything balanced.

At about four o'clock, the milesmen passed the railway house. Like most gangs, they worked an average of fifty hours a week, with shorter hours during the winter. They were on their way to leave the tools back and when they stopped the bogie, we climbed onto it. Since he was in good humour, my father was persuaded to let us have a jaunt on it as far as the hut, but we had to walk back ourselves.

CHAPTER SIX

Saturday Confession

Once a month, my mother was in the habit of going to Saturday Confession and somebody would drive her into town in the pony and trap. Women of her generation were very modest and none moreso than she. Getting ready to go out, she never put on any makeup. Instead, she swore by buttermilk, rubbing it onto her face as a kind of moisturiser. Then, standing up, she looked for her hat and particularly her long coat which she never went anywhere without. *'Show your leg to the country man'*, goes the line in the song. Well my mother wouldn't show anything to anybody.

One Saturday, Larry decided to drive us into town, but halfway he started to cod with my mother out of a sense of divilment. With a peal of laughter he tipped the whip up, caught the hat off her head and left her sitting with her hair exposed to the elements. Suddenly, a gust of wind knocked the hat off the end of the whip and it skipped down the Tullamore road. The two of us sat in the trap open-mouthed and watched Lar as he stopped the pony and stumbled to catch the hat before it blew away.

"Isn't that fella an awful *baileabhair* [fool]?" my mother said bemusedly.

On the way to town, we passed young people on bicycles and carts and traps of all descriptions. Then, near River Street, we overtook an old woman going into town on the tailboard of an ass's cart. She wore a cape tied in a knot around her head and the lazy smoke from a clay pipe drifted into the air. As we drew alongside her in our trap, a small dog sitting on the tailboard began to bark excitedly. Acknowledging us with a friendly wave, the old woman turned to it and shouted in a coarse voice, "Sit down you!"

Reaching Clara, we turned right at D.E. Williams' shop and clipped into Main Street – a thoroughfare that was poorly lit at night and could get very muddy in bad weather. The street was busy for that time of the afternoon and the pony tried hard to avoid people as they crossed the road in all directions.

The previous week, a lot of hard bargaining had been done outside the door of P.J. White's and the cattle left a terrible mess from standing outside the chapel. Mr Clavin, the Clerk, spent a whole morning cleaning it off with buckets of water and cursing the very idea of a fair. Fortunately for his counterpart in Ballycumber, it was only held there on the second of May and everyone knew the cant:

The first of May, the first of summer,
The second of May, the fair of Ballycumber.

On Fair Day, an old scales was also erected on the roadside near the chemist's shop. Usefully enough, the bearded owner, Michael Pettitt, also stocked medicine for animals and went out regularly to farmers' houses on calls.

Alongside the regular fair business, there were various kinds of hawkers plying their trade. One man sold second-hand clothes and there were musicians of all descriptions. When he had some money, my father used to take an empty creel with him and might return with a new pig or some fowl for my mother.

Today was a little quieter however and we left the trap in White's yard, along with those of the other country people.

"Make sure and tie that pony well, *a Mhic* [Son]," my mother cautioned. With a careful hand, Larry tethered the animal and with a wave strolled out of the yard and down Main Street. Meanwhile, I linked my mother's arm and we made our way across the dusty road to Clyne's open-fronted butcher's shop.

On either side of the premises hung various sides of beef and pork, jutting onto the street on iron cranes. Inside, past the breeze-jolted meat, stood a wooden chopping board and a wicker basket to receive the off-cuts and offal. I thought that my mother was buying half the shop, because she asked Sam Clyne to wrap a whole pound of sausages, ham and other meats to last her the week. My father was very fond of eating *cruibíns* [pig's trotters], so she also made sure to ask the butcher for plenty of those.

When the meat was parcelled, Sam, who was his usual witty self, leaned across the chopping board and beckoned to us. 'Wait till I tell you ladies. Did ye ever hear about the time the lad from Clashawaun tried to get the better of me?'

"Oh now wait," my mother replied in mock horror. "You needn't tell me anything. I know it already."

Delighted by this reaction, the moustachioed butcher grinned from ear to ear and continued with the yarn.

"Your man says, 'I knew you Mr Clyne, when you hadn't an arse in your trousers.' 'Did you now?' says I. 'Well I've still got the same arse but there are three or four pairs of trousers for it now!'"

Shaking with laughter, the butcher's son Frank put the parcel of meat onto the scales and weighed it out. After making up the bill in a little book with its columns for pounds, shillings and pence, he wiped his hands on his apron and brought the meat over to our trap. He had fallen madly in love and lost no opportunity to see me.

If my mother had an inkling, she never let on. In the evening, she used to read her prayers from a little prayer book in which she had decorated all the saints in brightly coloured foil. Sometimes, seeing a lone cyclist passing the house, she would stop praying and look out the window to exclaim, "There's Frank Clyne passing, and he's looking in!"

Frank was watching to see if there was any sign of me coming out. He was a nice boy but he was also a flirt, and could meet me and then go and meet someone else the next night. I'd cod with him but there was nothing serious about it.

After packing the meat away, we went into the Grocery end of White's to buy a two-pound pot of jam, a box of custard and a new mantle for the lamp. Frowning, I held the latter. The mantle, made of muslin, was in my opinion a dangerous yoke and I eyed it with suspicion. Meanwhile, my mother who was not the haggling type, paid over the money asked for.

Afterwards, we were taken into the kitchen where the apron-garbed maid, who was a masterhand at baking, gave us tea and some of her own brown bread. Mrs White regarded my mother as a valued customer, particularly since she was one of the Burkes from Kilmucklin. It wasn't every trap or car that came into the yard that got tea from her, or else she might be feeding people for a month!

A Keaney by birth, she had taken over much of the running of the business after her husband Michael Henry White sustained a back injury playing hurling. He was bedridden above the pub for three and a half years and was unable to attend to the customers at all. Fortunately, his wife was very capable.

There was a big office at the back where she used to keep her books. Besides weekly orders of beer and spirits arriving from Dublin by train, there were many accounts to be reconciled, particularly deliveries of pig meal into the yard and hardware items such as shovels. Besides the bar and grocery staff, several locals were employed as yardsmen and their wages needed to be calculated. On top of this, there were the seasonal demands of local people who put in large orders at Christmas and Easter. It was also quite normal for the shop to keep running tabs, especially with farming families. These amounts were usually paid in full around March, when those customers had sold their cattle.

When she was finished, Mrs White came out to us.

"Will you take a drop of whiskey?" she asked.

"Musha no, I won't," my mother replied – herself not much of a drinker. "I'd only take a drop meh'be at Christmas time."

Sitting heavily into a wooden chair, the businesswoman prodded a poker into the fire and smiled at me indulgently.

"How is poor Kathleen since the Dunne girl passed away?" she asked, her eyes moving away to meet those of my mother.

"Ah, it was a shocking thing to happen," my mother began. "Father Bracken broke the news above at Saturday Mass. But sure Kathleen is alright, aren't you *a Mhuirnín* [Dear]?"

I nodded to reassure her and sipped my tea quietly. Soon, the conversation moved onto other matters.

There was no getting over consumption, and both my mother and Mrs White knew it. Of course, my mother would hit the ceiling if she knew that Popsie had given me her shawl to wear shortly before she died. Despite the rainy night, Tommy Feehan demanded that I take it off, and chided that I shouldn't be wearing anything belonging to that unfortunate girl.

When we came out from our visit with Mrs White, we walked up the street to St Brigid's Church for confession. As I sat quietly thinking about poor Popsie, my mother whispered to me in the pew that she wanted a new pair of shoes. When we came out of the church we had nothing to do but walk straight across the road.

"Come on over and we'll get them," I said. "But you'll have to fit them on."

A look of horror came over her face.

"I'm not taking off my shoes!" she cried. "You can bring me

home a pair, because the assistant will see my foot!"

In those days, women like my mother used to wear long dresses that went down to their ankles and everything was covered. If it was me, I'd take off my shoes at any stage. So I said back to her, "Sure he'll have to see your foot to fit on the shoe!"

But she was very stubborn and refused to go in.

Instead, I had to grudgingly cross the street and go into Egan's on my own. As soon as the little bell chimed above the door, a shop assistant appeared on the narrow stairs. When he saw who it was, he came down to see what I wanted.

"What size is she, Cath?" he asked.

I stood like a half clown and looked at him.

"Begod I don't know," I replied.

"What about a size six?" he ventured.

After that, I was bringing shoes home from Clara for a month until I got the right fit!

CHAPTER SEVEN

"Don't be Ugly" Says Oul' Jack Ugan

Part of my father's duty was to maintain the crossing adjacent to our house, but he couldn't always be there to man it. Because of this, there was a weathered sign near the gates that carried a warning:

G.S. & W.R. NOTICE
Any person leaving this gate open
Is liable to a penalty of 40 shillings

In the normal course of events, a farmer coming to the crossing would grab the reins to stop the car, open the 'high' gate, then cross the railway to open the 'low' one on the far side. For pedestrian traffic, stone stiles were built into the wall. Mishaps during crossings were rare and the gates were never locked, even at night, despite my father holding keys for them.

That meant of course that it was up to any farmer who wanted to cross over to the bog road to take good care, but my father's patience was severely tested with Jack Wogan. One evening, he came down the lane singing and as drunk as an owl. Worn out by his efforts, he lay down to let the pony make the rest of the journey, but half way down the hill, one of the wheels came off his cart and the poor pony had to drag it along with one shaft scraping against the ground.

When he reached the crossing gates, he climbed down.

"Get out Gaynor, and open this gate," he demanded noisily.

Hearing the familiar strains of his lurid neighbour, my father tutted in annoyance.

"Wouldn't that Ugan fella give you peregrinations altogether?" he said to my mother, scarcely hiding his delight at the unexpected opportunity to use his favourite word. My mother just sighed and went back to her prayer book. Both waited for Wogan to quieten down and open the gate himself.

But after a few minutes had passed with no sign of any let up, my father lost his patience.

"God dammit," he shouted, standing up abruptly from the fire. "He's an oul' fella gone in the head!"

He strode across the kitchen and threw back the front door. A sliver of light fell across the matted features and dishevelled shirt of our neighbour. As my father walked towards him, an air of triumph played drunkenly on his face, but it quickly turned to helpless dismay when he realised that assistance was the last thing on the ganger's mind. Ignoring Wogan, he strode past him, uncoupled the pony from the car and rammed the vehicle into the ditch on its one remaining wheel. His temper appeased, he stamped back into the house and slammed the door behind him.

Despite the fact that nobody was hurt, Wogan was dumbfounded. He stood in the laneway for a few minutes, looking down at his hapless car, then towards the house and then back up the lane. Eventually he conceded defeat, climbed over the stile and staggered home. The next morning however he reported the incident to police Constable Walsh, claiming that my father had neglected his duty.

The rule of law was that any complaint for the neglect of level crossing gates had to be made within the space of a month. Weekly Petty Sessions were held for the highway and it was only at these that issues concerning railway property could be considered.

The Courthouse was next to the church at the top of the town and James Perry Goodbody from Inchmore House was the judge presiding. When he stood to face the court, Wogan explained what had happened. He wanted my father to open the gate and shut it when farmers were coming. That would make my father a real 'oul' egit' altogether.

A barrister stood to speak in defence of my father.

"Your honour, I would like to remind the Court of a case that was brought before the Ballinamore Petty Sessions in 1890." Clearing his throat, the barrister continued. "A man named John Sheridan had been charged with having trespassed onto the railway with a donkey loaded with creels between two farm level crossings. Since the argument was offered that a man employed at the crossing could not possibly be at hand twenty-four hours a day to operate the gates, the case was dismissed."

"Very well," Goodbody answered, "but nevertheless, if the man responsible for the crossing is found to be wantonly negligent, some recompense has to be made."

The judge looked gravely at my father and then at Wogan.

"Weighing the facts presented to me, I am left with no alternative but to award full payment for a case of this type. The amount due is set at £5 precisely. Case dismissed."

The hammer rose and fell and Wogan was delighted.

When he heard the verdict, my father was extremely put out, and naturally there was a falling out over it. In fact, Jack's attempt to pacify my father with 'Don't be ugly' became a cant amongst us then as children, and we used to say it at every opportunity.

A few months later, Wogan got greedy and decided to push his case for a bigger payout. He thought that by bringing my father to court a second time, he would be forced to stay opening and shutting the gate all day, but, James Goodbody just glared at him angrily.

"Wogan," he bellowed, "since you got the money, you got too big for your boots!"

To my father's immense satisfaction, the case against him this time was dismissed.

CHAPTER EIGHT

The Convent School

As we stooped amongst the potato drills, Liz Doorley stood up to straighten her back. "Lord God Cahy!' she exclaimed, "Sure we're doing all the mullicking for them oul' wans."

"That's because them townie wans are all swanky grand," I added with a look of envy on my dirt-streaked face.

Having walked to the Sisters of Mercy School on the Kilbeggan Road, we were now busy picking potatoes. That morning I had waited, shivering in my hand-me-down coat, at the end of the path for Liz to come down the line. I could see her house from my own window. All summer long, we played together, sliding on jute sacks and climbing up trees, but now the autumn had come. It was time to go to school whenever the weather or our chores would allow.

"And do yeh know," Liz said, inspecting one of the potatoes with a beady eye, "I was pegged out today with n'er a lunch nor no bread nor nothin'!"

"Begod, I like your coat," she exclaimed, suddenly noticing what I was wearing.

"Ah thanks," I replied.

The coat had come from Ciss and I gazed wanly as pieces of collar fur blew all over the potato field. Underneath, I wore a striped pinafore that had been handed down to me from my elder sister Bab. In order to make it fit, my mother made me stand on a chair the evening before while she turned up a few inches from the bottom. For shoes, I was given a pair of old 'button boots' that

Bab had also cast off. When the leather was stiff and new, an iron object known as a 'buttoner' had been employed to draw the buttons through the holes but by the time they came down to me, the hide had become so worn that I was able to do them up without difficulty.

Earlier that morning, we had skipped up the lane to Norah Bergin's house to see if she was ready. Inside, the kitchen smelled of dry ashes from last night's fire and her father, Oul' Tim and the mother lay fast asleep in the settle bed beside it. Oul' Tim was a pig dealer from Laois, and you'd know only to look at him that his wife was twenty years his junior. With his white beard nodding, he was the nearest thing I ever saw to Santy Claus. I whispered in to Norah, "Are you ready?"

Once she had gathered up her things, we strolled past still-green hedges and byways until we arrived at the New Road where the Dignam family lived. We had to collect a classmate there but on account of her being an only child, she was always delayed.

Other girls were walking from the other side of Clara, from Tobar and other places. If we were late, penance entailed a long stand in the corner facing the wall, so you can imagine how monotonous that was. You'd be left in that corner long enough to make a hole in the floor.

"Go on you Cat, and see if she's ready," Liz said, ushering me towards the door.

Peering into the kitchen, I could see that the girl's grandmother had fetched a stool, upon which a comb was placed. The other girls joined me at the half door and we watched impatiently as the old woman slowly brushed out the knots in the little girl's hair. When she was finished, she offered her cheek for a kiss. Suddenly, Liz's voice cut coarsely through the happy family scene.

"Ah, will you kiss her arse," she shouted. "We'll be late for school!"

The school building comprised of one main classroom with high windows, next to which stood the convent and a laundry. The different classes shared the same room, with a divider for the older girls at one end but when the weather was fine, we were taught in a field with high trees for shade. Apart from a dry lavatory there were no toilets, so a man was paid to come regularly to the school with a horse and cart to clean it out. When he arrived at the gates, he used to unhitch the cart and wash everything down with a barrel of water.

We were country girls, so the Sisters had us earmarked for the job of picking vegetables on their own land. They left the town girls such Patricia Cowen and Mary Daly alone, because their parents owned public houses and a shop in Clara. Bridget White, who was very well liked, was probably too small and dainty for picking potatoes. Doted on by all, she was nicknamed 'Robin' White. Likewise, May Sheridan was never sent out because her father was earning more than twenty shillings a week for his job as head porter at Clara Station.

Beside us stooped Popsie Dunne, who, despite living in the town, did not have a father high up enough to excuse her from potato-picking. The Dunnes lived in River Street and Popsie's father, who had a lame leg, tended a garden that belonged to Goodbodys. Surrounded by a high wall, the garden, which was as big as a whole half field, was kept well hidden. To enter it, you went through a wooden side door and I loved to play there. It was full of blackcurrants, apple trees, roses and flowering shrubs and I thought it was like the Garden of Eden.

At lunchtime, starving and with big red cheeks from the fresh air, we were taken down to the front gate and given a master feed of potatoes in the laundry room attached to the convent. The place was full of the smell of clean linen and was very warm on account of the big range. We used to have our cookery class in there too

– learning how to make fancy food that was a cut above what we might get at home.

Sitting at the table, I wondered how it would feel to be like one of the town girls because they were all dressed up. I imagined that in Clara everyone would see you in your best clothes, and that walking down the street all done up must be the grandest thing.

In the afternoon, needlework was taught by Sister Aquinas. Like the other nuns who ran the school, she was dressed in a habit with nothing out but her face and she wore a cross on her chest. Around her waist, she kept another cross, suspended from a tight sock of leather. You could get a wallop of that for hardly any reason at all.

The nun had been quite fond of my eldest sister, because as a schoolgirl she had great hands for crocheting and made lovely tablecloths. I had no skill for it at all, whereas Ciss showed some flair and would sew if the nuns had never taught her. With nerves, the sweat rolled off me because I kept balling up the material until the next thing, the ball was blacker than me.

Then, out of a sense of frustration, I splashed some ink out of the well and it landed on the clean frock of the girl in front. When she turned around, I pretended to concentrate on my crochet. I knew that the homemade concoction of the nuns' would never wash out. When she noticed what I had done, Sister Aquinas pulled the jaw out of me and muttered, "You're not a bit like your sister! Go over there now and stand in that corner."

When Father Bracken arrived, he took one disapproving look in my direction.

"Are you standing in the corner again Kathleen?" he reprimanded. I hated that, and would rather have been slapped than suffer the embarrassment.

"Well feck my sister," I muttered under my breath. But you see, the nuns were like oul' maids; cross with everyone and I was sure that they were that way simply because they had no man.

We came home after school to find my mother serving up a big pan of fish in the middle of a load of spuds. We always got fish on a Friday because nobody was supposed to eat meat. The sea was miles away from us but we were well looked after by Mick Goldsbury from River Street. He visited my mother with a big barrel full of water and herrings. Because he was the only Jew living in Clara, he never went by any name other than 'Micky the Jew'. Sometimes, we used to hear him on the boreen asking people for their wool or 'vool' as he called it, and he sold that on as a sideline. I don't know where he used to get the fish, but he made a good living selling it. It puts me in mind of a saying that the old people had: 'Sup in the soup and leave the herring for your Daddy'. That was a reminder of the old times in Clara when people often made a soup of boiled herring. Only the head of the house was allowed to eat the piece of fish, whereas the rest had to make do with dipping their potatoes into the soup.

At suppertime we got Indian meal, which my mother called 'Indian Bocht' or 'Bochta'. It was a kind of reddish grain from which she made stirabout with plenty of buttermilk. Sometimes, she might put a lump of butter in the middle with a caution: "Make sure and eat enough now childer, because I'm not doing any more for ye tonight!"

One morning in October, Larry and I went up the road looking for puddles. In those days the roads were often neglected and after a night of rain, all the holes were filled with what we called 'lotts' of water. We wetted one another a little way off up the laneway and then made a plan to say it was spilling rain and we couldn't go to school. My mother, looking out at us coming back of a lovely mild morning exclaimed, "The Lord bless us; I didn't think it was raining!"

CHAPTER NINE

On to the High School

On the morning of my confirmation – a Saturday – the nuns were very busy in Clara chapel trying to organise things. I sat nervously in my white confirmation dress and watched all my school friends as they walked up the aisle to be questioned by Bishop Lawrence. I had picked Mary as my Confirmation name and felt very grown up that, despite being just twelve, my parents had allowed me to choose it for myself.

All through third class, I had been taught by Sister Bernadette, and one day she came into the class with tickets coloured blue, red and yellow. The purpose of this was to grade us according to how well we knew our Catechism. Blue was the best that anyone could do, whereas yellow meant that you were just barely getting there.

A few years before, Bab did herself proud by getting a red ticket. As Tommie was washing at the outdoor pump on the morning of his confirmation, a chip of red paint fell into the water and lo and behold, he got a ticket the same colour. They were tops, and I was determined to do just as well.

Soon it was my turn and the old nun tapped me on the head. Galloping away in my head were the Six Precepts of the Church and the Ten Commandments, but when I got to the Bishop, the simplicity of his question threw me off guard: "How many persons are there in one God?"

"Three."

"And can you name them?"

"Well, for one start off there's God and then his Son."
Leaning forward, the Bishop tapped me on the cheek:
"And who is the third?"
"God's wife I suppose."

Then the old man held out his hand – I kissed his ring like I had been told, and was given a yellow ticket. I came home with it hanging off me like a half clown.

Later, when I reached fifth class, I realised that there were worse things in life than not getting a blue ticket. One morning, as one of the girls was leaving to go to the toilet, she tripped over a bag and a compact rolled out. The compact belonged to May Sheridan but since she wouldn't own up, Sister Bernadette put the blame on me. As she marched me to the top of the room, the whole class sat looking at me, wondering what was going to happen next and whether there was going to be a scene. I duly obliged. As the nun began to lord it over me in front of the girls, I felt a wave of temper building. "It's not my bag!" I shouted.

I ran out of the classroom and didn't stop until I reached home. When I came into the kitchen I pleaded my case to my mother.

"I'm not going to that oul' school anymore," I panted, "over the bag!"

But my mother, who was getting the dinner ready said, "I don't know what you're talking about *a Lana*."

"The fecking oul' bag," I persisted. "It belongs to t'oul' Sheridan wan." May was a daughter of John Sheridan who worked as Head Porter in Clara Station, and the nuns were very great with him which made her a favourite. I knew that and couldn't explain it to my mother, but I tried to tell her the best way I could.

The next day, the nuns came out to see her. Unsurprisingly, the turkeys in the yard nearly went out of their minds when they heard their starched habits rattling down the hill and nobody could blame them.

You see, those same nuns were used to people bowing to them on the path or standing out on the road to let them pass. On summer evenings, their constitutional walk often took them past the railway house where a big card game might be in session. Everything would get fired to the ceiling when the ramblers heard the rattle of the nuns' habits, and I used to have an awful job trying to right chairs and pick up all the cards before they knocked at the door. From their hiding places in the two bedrooms on either side of the hearth, Ned Robbins and the rest of the players would peer at them around the edge of the door and through the keyhole until they left.

Now here they were coming down the lane, but this time it was me who was going to get the works.

"Jesus," I said to my mother, "Those oul' bitches are here but I'm still not going to school!"

The following Sunday, I found out why the nuns were so determined to get me back, especially since they had let other girls go before. The priest informed us from the pulpit that a private Intermediate teacher called Mrs Molloy had come to Clara, and he cautioned our parents not to send their children to her. The nuns didn't want her school and they went out of their way to take her character, because she was taking pupils away from them. Ignoring the priest, my father – heedless in his own way – gave the money to my mother and asked her to deal with the teacher.

New pupils began to arrive daily and soon they were coming from rock and briar on bikes. In spite of what the priest said, the new school was a smashing place. Mrs Molloy gave lessons in music and book-keeping. Above all, she taught typing, which was essential because with that skill a lot of girls could take up clerical positions until they got married. I boasted at home that I was getting Intermediate education.

When I close my eyes, I can see it still. Oul' Jack Molloy, who was a taxi driver, couldn't be any more different from his well-educated wife and he often stood out on the roadway as we were coming up the hill. With his wife in mind, he used to sing these comical lines:

> *I can't change her,*
> *And neither will I try,*
> *But I'll put her up for auction,*
> *In the street by and by.*

Jack never used bad language, but whenever he had an urge to curse, he used to say by way of politeness, 'Oh that's the curse.' That was probably just as bad, since he had the curse in his mind but wouldn't say it.

Once I had learnt the basics of book-keeping from Mrs Molloy and received a certificate for playing the violin, my father got me off to Birr to serve my time to grocery. Now in the name of Jaysus, how could you serve your time to grocery? I was serving my time to a few oul' bags of sugar! The shop sold all sorts of things and once a week, the owner who was called Ms Kenny, had a visit from her brother who was in the habit of leaving his pony and trap in the little yard behind the shop.

I was going with a boy at the time called Tommy Ronan, and he used to cycle all the way from Clara to see me. Unfortunately, it was difficult for us to meet in private because the old woman who ran the shop wouldn't let me out unless she was coming too. At half five every evening, when I had finished weighing and parcelling the sugar into little 1lb bags, she used to lock the door and we'd go for our little walk. That broke my heart when I thought of the lovely chap I had at home.

Our route took us away from the town, out into the country and the old woman muttered to herself the whole way. Perhaps she felt responsible for me because I was serving my time with her. Although she never said it outright, I suspected that she worried about me becoming pregnant, but she needn't have feared because when I was with her no one could touch me. She came with me everywhere and almost followed me into the toilet. I'd say that that was prison and didn't I know it so one day I said to myself: 'I'm getting out of here.'

The grocery shop was up a laneway at the back end of the town, but I was lodged in and had to stay put for the time being. It wasn't long before an opportunity presented itself.

As luck would have it, there was a middle-aged man stopping in the same shop who used to go around farmyards collecting feathers. His name was Bunkum and I asked him one evening if he would give me a lift home in his van to Ashfield. He agreed and after coming home with him, I stayed put and never went back to Birr.

CHAPTER TEN

"Oh Jaysus, Have You a Ma?"

As the 'bicycle' trundled towards milepost 65¾, the steady click of its iron wheels against the rail made it sound like a slow engine. On board the converted bogie lay a keying hammer, six detonators, a red flag and a lighted hand signal lamp for tunnels. Beside these lay a few key packings and other essential tools.

At the front, a milesman pedalled frantically – his waistcoat flapping open in the breeze whilst behind him lounged Inspector J. O'Neill and a colleague. They frequently took notes and made comments on the state of the line, but as the bicycle neared the Ballinough Hills, the inspector suddenly closed his notebook and shouted, 'Stop her there.' When the wheels had ground to a halt, the three men climbed off their leather saddles and stepped onto the embankment.

The milesman waited quietly while O'Neill and the other man took more notes and talked amongst themselves. Without a glance in the milesman's direction, the inspector held his hand out.

"Hand me that permanent way gauge," he said.

When the milesman obliged, the two men carefully measured the distance between the tracks.

"The gauge of that road is alright, but you can see where she's not level," O'Neill said.

Taking out his notebook, he carefully wrote 'subsidence' in block letters and observed the location.

Later on, my father, returning along the cycle track from Clara

Station, put his gang to work to ensure that the fault was rectified in advance of the afternoon train. Where the sleeper had sunk, a jack was used to lever it off the ground and then a special type of trowel was used to fill the space underneath. This was important because if one sleeper was lower than its neighbour, the fishplate was more likely to crack at the joint. If that went unnoticed, the chair would become loose, the keys would fall out and eventually there would be a derailment.

The men worked on until the one o'clock call to down tools came. There was just one official dinner hour, but an unofficial break was also taken at ten in the morning which the gang sometimes had to go into a field to take.

On this occasion however, the bicycles were parked against the wall of the hut nestled in the lee side of the esker and one of the men produced some old 'keys' from inside the hut. Coated with creosote, the compressed wooden blocks were sure to burn far longer than ordinary tinder. As a result, they were often kept for lighting fires at the hut and some men took them home with them. Soon a good fire was blazing, and the kettle was placed carefully over it on a tripod.

As the Milesmen sat down to tea, an old woman called Sarah Daly shuffled into view around the bend in the track. In a district without straight roads, the Clara-Tullamore railway was the easiest way to go to town and it had very few turns. Since it wasn't a mainline railway, everyone used it and farmers only stopped short of driving their cattle along it. But although the G.S.R. posted notices on every second or third telegraph post warning the public against trespassing, my father had no intention of enforcing the company rule.

Sarah lived with her mother and both had hair as white as snow – so white in fact that you wouldn't know one from the other. To make things worse, she never wore a hat and her hair was half way between long and short, giving her a wild appearance. Both women used the line to walk into Clara, and on this occasion Mrs Daly had gone before her daughter by about an hour.

Sitting with my father was a young milesman called John Keaney and as she came alongside the gang, Sarah turned to him and enquired, "Did you see me ma?" He looked up but when he saw the old woman who was doing the asking, the edges of his mouth curled into a bemused smile.

"Oh Jaysus!" he exclaimed. "Have you a ma?"

The same John Keaney was a farmer's only son. One Saturday he was helping his neighbour and cousin, Pat Keaney, to draw hay near Cool Na Hiley when the pony shied at something and ran away. John jumped out and tried to reach the pony's head to stop it from bolting onto the railway but the shaft of the car hit him in the stomach, killing him instantly. There was a big scene that day and a group of men had to go over to the field. They carried the body home on the back of a cart covered by a white sheet and when his poor mother saw that she lost her head altogether. She never got over it and blamed her nephew personally. I remember her confronting him many years afterwards with the accusation: "Pat Keaney, you killed my son," which wasn't fair because they had only been helping each other.

Like poor John, my father also had a lot of work to do on Saturday. When he wasn't doing repairs at home or getting the pony shod, he was sowing potatoes, turnips, parsnips, onions and other vegetables, and he used to pay a neighbour to open up the drills.

When the potato stalks were six inches high, he prepared a mix of bluestone and washing soda and sprayed the fledgling crops with it. As a child I often lay down between the tall, leafy shoots, sure that I could stay there until tomorrow without being missed.

In the evening, with help from the lads, the men brought in a big cartload for pitting at home in the Railway House. Having spent all day doing hay over near the field where they were growing, they would fill up the cart and leave them standing in a bag in the kitchen. It was important to get enough seed potatoes so that we could grow some more for the next season and my mother had the job of cutting out the eyes. A handful of potatoes would hardly be out of the clay when someone would say: 'Would you ever go for a bucket of turnips?' We didn't think of shops then.

For milk, we kept a goat tethered outside. Drivers and firemen used to call them the 'Milesman's Cow', because to many families living in railway houses across the length and breadth of the country, that's what they were. When she had eaten all the grass around her in a circle, somebody would say, 'Go up and move that goat.' That involved a walk up the railway embankment to take the wooden stake out of the ground and move it somewhere further down where there was more grass. In return, we got great milk, but although my father swore by it in a cup of tea, I never liked it. Oul' Ned Robbins used to say that if you drank goat's milk and ran against the wind, it would make your hair go curly. We laughed at that because the old people were full of piserogs or superstitions.

We always had enough to eat, thanks to the hard work of our parents, but in those days people were very self-sufficient in many other ways besides the growing of food. One such example was in the provision of shoes, which my father couldn't afford to buy. Instead, he used to buy a big lump of leather and sole them himself. At the rate we went through them, we were all the time being shod like horses.

I often watched curiously as he laid the tools out in front of him. First he scattered a handful of brass tacks across the table. Next he fetched an awl – a small pointed tool used to punch holes in the leather. Through that he threaded a big needle attached to a leathery lace made of hemp that had been softened in a basin of water. In order to get the right shape for his piece of leather, he used a last for the size of the foot. He used to put the shoe on that and cut his leather to shape. There was a small last, a middle-sized one and then a man's size.

Since we had no last of our own, we were obliged to borrow one from our neighbours. In the house where we used to go for it, there lived an oul' farmer called Johnny Mac who was dying for ages. Any time my mother went out to enquire about him, the answer would come back, "Ah, he's on the last." That meant the last straw of the dying. One day, I remember my mother saying, "Will some of ye go down to Macs and get the last?"

We were sent to do everything and weren't allowed to grow up but it didn't do us a bit of harm. I can still see my father laughing, because I used to say the quarest things. In frustration I had shouted, "I'm not going, because Johnny's sitting on it!"

CHAPTER ELEVEN

Visitors to the House

My mother always had an uncanny knack of predicting a visitor's arrival. If she dropped a fork during the course of her daily chores, she used to say, "Oh, there's a lady coming to the house," and sure enough, some lady was bound to arrive at the door. When a knife was dropped, that meant that a man was going to call. I never believed in those oul' piserogs, but if he was working nearby, my father often came home for lunch.

Once, he brought a man called John Moylan with him and in expectation of their arrival, my mother made 'boxty' – a type of potato bread. The griddle upon which the cake sat was a round flat piece of iron on coals and instead of using a knife, she used a length of string to cut it into four squares.

When the men arrived, my mother chatted to John for a while but there was no sign of the food.

Eventually my father shouted, "God dammit, are you giving the man nothing to eat? Sure he must be lepping i' the ground with the hunger."

The milesman was delighted then to get a feed off the griddle and he wagged his leg at the table in a contented sort of way.

As the tea was being poured, my mother looked for news.

"Do you ever see oul' Dunbar this weather?" she enquired politely.

"Ah sure Mrs Gaynor, he done the bould thing," John replied.

"The Lord save us," she said. 'What's the world coming to at all?"

My father gave the milesman a cautionary look.

"Well John, if t'Inspector is guilty of anything, 'tis a brave man would say a word about it," he said flatly.

My mother gave him a weary look.

"Arra, there'd be no bad min if it wasn't for bad women," she sighed.

Another time, the same Joe Burke, who had been so busy with his 't'inkin' – toddled down the line during lunch hour. My father, who was working very near the house, had come in to get a proper meal. There was a long bench or 'form' pulled out in front of the fire which helped to keep the draft away and he took off his brown boots to warm his feet.

After a while, he got up from the hearth, slipped his boots on loosely and peered into the pot that my mother had on the crane. This time, she had made Colcannon, the principal ingredient of which was potatoes, mashed with a stick called a 'Beatle'.

"Begob, I wouldn't ate that now in a fit," he said, replacing the lid with a cloth. Without further comment, he lifted the latch and walked out the back door. Soon, we could see him through the window, taking long strides past the sheds in an attempt to work up an appetite. He never ate unless he was hungry.

Eventually, he returned indoors, his laces trailing behind him and announced to my mother, "Well do you know what missus? I have an edge on me now."

But he had hardly lifted the fork to his mouth when the latch lifted and Joe Burke came into the kitchen and sat down. God help my father. He had started to eat a lovely dinner that his wife had cooked for him, but while Joe was talking, he picked away off the plate.

"God, I travelled the world Mr Gaynor," he announced idly.

"Did you?" my father replied with a slightly irritated expression.

"I did, because you know," continued Joe, chewing loudly, "I travelled to Ballycumber one time for my two sisters." The funny thing was that Ballycumber was only a few miles from Clara. It was only a one-horse town. There might not even be one horse in it.

My father gave the linesman a wallop with his fork.

"Well," he snapped. 'No matter what travelling you're doing, don't be eating my dinner!"

At other times of the day we often got people selling things. Tinkers, for instance used to arrive in the locality in horse-drawn caravans. Their favourite place to camp was in a sheltered byroad, away from the wind and rain. They used to build a big fire there and stay for two or three days until somebody in town made a complaint and the guards came to shift them.

Once they had settled in, the women would come around the houses selling paper flowers bound with wire. One winter's day some children belonging to the McDonaghs gathered around the door, pleading, "Let us warm me hands missus," and "Give us a bit of bread".

When I ran back into the kitchen to tell my mother that the tinkers were at the door, they called after me, "We're not tinkers – we're travellers." Then she buttered some bread and allowed them to come in to put their hands to the fire.

Another unfortunate nicknamed the 'Scelper' Brian used to come in during the afternoon and I often heard my mother say, "I want to give him a bit of dinner now." The Scelper's fighting days had long since ended and as he sat at the table he was barely able to take a bit of stew. He'd be gone by the time my father came home.

My mother had great charity, considering the view commonly held that if you didn't own land, you were nobody. She understood that more than most, especially since my father was just a workman on the railway. As the saying goes, she didn't believe in rubbing fat on a fat pig's arse. On the other hand, there were farmers in those days, who, when the dinner hour came would be brought into the parlour room to get everything handed to them. The poor workman who deserved it most would get what was left over.

We knew two workmen living near us who had a similar experience with the Kellys. To their dismay, they found that after a tough first day, they were hardly fed. Both were falling out of their standing. Afterwards Kelly, holding a storm lantern, ushered them out to an outhouse where they were shown a bit of straw to sleep on. Neither could sleep for the hunger, so they stood there, caught between a rock and a hard place. All they could think of to soften their appetites was the big plate of laughing spuds they were sure to get at Robbins's place.

As the glow of Kelly's lantern disappeared back across the yard, both men agreed that this was worse than purgatory. Making the best of his lot, the older of the two, who was a bit of a philosopher, lit his pipe and stretched out on the straw. As he drew on the lighted tobacco, he said, 'This is surely a place where souls suffer for a time before they can go to John Robbins!'

During the week, the milk carts made their usual rounds. Our milkman, Jockins, would do the town first, serving the people in Clashawaun before turning his pony towards the rural hinterland. Once, he took his two young sons with him and when they arrived at our house, they ran inside. Meanwhile, their father took the milk from the tin with a little tilly and handed it to my mother.

The boys had begged their mother to allow them to come to Gaynors' because they loved my mother's griddle bread. Her cooking implements in those days included a cast-iron skillet, griddle and pot oven, and the food had the taste of the fire in it. The griddle might be placed on one of those little piles of embers and the iron took the heat quickly and kept it for a long time. Occasionally you might have to heat it again with another ember from the hearth. In the middle of cooking, the cake was turned to harn on the other side and when the youngest lad came in; my mother took it up and gave him some of it. It was like a big wheel of a car, but because she only went half way, he said, 'Mrs Gaynor; ye're a shocking dacent woman, but you should have went out the whole way with the cake!'

Meanwhile, the eldest boy stood with his hands behind his back, telling a story about a cow calving. He was a divil for talking and didn't notice that the little boy was getting impatient until eventually, despairing of ever getting a word in, he shouted, "Would you ever shut up and let a man talk!"

In his surprise, the big lad fell silent and allowed his brother to speak. The story was about getting up in the middle of the night and holding a lamp. In those days, it was a natural procedure for a cow to lie down in a field near a drain and start giving birth. As the cow lay on the ground, the boys experienced the sight of the cow giving life to another life, which very few city people would see. A crowd of men carrying lamps ran to the field then and dragged the calf away to safety because the minute the animal was born; its first instinct was to stand up.

After calving, a cow's milk was always different for a while. From that changed milk, my mother made beasting pudding – a food that was going out of fashion when I was young. Beasting milk was lovely to taste, because it was so different from ordinary milk. It was very rich and had a different colour in it for a couple of days, until the cow returned to normal. My mother would put that in a baker and heat it over the fire until it curdled. You could nearly cut it then with a knife. You put sugar on it and the final result was beasting pudding.

Besides the two lads who delivered the milk, another regular visitor was a man called Mike Donohue. The Donohues were a lovely family, and in particular the sister was very holy, but Mike himself was a bit wild. He used to snare rabbits and the occasional pheasant near Doury wood and then sell them to all the neighbours around for beer. Arriving out to our house, he would come in on the back door carrying a stick on his back with a brace of rabbits hanging from it.

My mother often bought two for four pence each, but she wouldn't let Mike go until he cleaned them. With a mischievous smile, he would ask her for the long-handled knife and the knife-box, which she kept in the dresser. The knife box was really a kind of whetstone and as he drew the blade back and forth on it, the edge became sharp. When he was satisfied, Mike would pull a chair up to the table and remove the insides and fur from the rabbits. While he worked, my mother would grease the three-legged iron baker in preparation for roasting them on the hearth.

As well as using traps, Mike kept a ferret onto which he tied a muzzle before sending down rabbit holes. One day, I was in the little wash place cleaning it down when my mother came running in the back door shouting and wringing her hands in terror. Convinced that she had said, "Here's a spirit, here's a spirit," I nearly leapt out of my skin. I thought that a ghost had appeared, when in actual fact what had happened was that Mike's ferret had escaped from its cage and was slinking around our yard in its collar. Of course, my mother thought I was after losing my head when I ran too!

In those days, housewives were very busy looking after their large families and often needed the services of a washerwoman. On washday, which was usually Monday, Posie Bannon would come in to wash for my mother for a couple of hours before moving on to the next house. In the absence of an indoor sink or taps, she kept a washboard with two handles on either side and, knowing that Posie was expected, she would heat a big, black pot of water over the fire.

As she made her way through the locality, Posie often met her son, Georgie Bannon, who was a thatcher. Like his mother, Georgie was a familiar sight to us as he cycled from job to job with his bag of tools – a long straw rake, thatching hooks and needles, spars, an eaves knife and a pair of shears. Oat straw was generally used in our locality and the thatcher went from the eaves to the roof up to the ridge, starting on the left and moving along that way like reading a book.

Wherever Georgie was thatching, Posie would arrive in fliggits, which meant that her clothes were scanty and torn. One windy afternoon, she came out to him with a bottle of tea and she'd hardly any clothes on her as usual. She looked up at him and shouted, "Here I am Georgie and I'm ready to fly!"

Georgie, who was in the middle of tying scallops down in rows to hold the new thatch, looked down off the ladder at her.

"Well Jaysus," he said in exasperation. "When you rise that you may never 'light'!"

Unlike his mother, Georgie was all dressed up with nowhere to go. He was terribly swanky, which was understandable since thatchers could earn a lot of money for their craft. On top of that, he had my father beat for wearing chains and watches. The funny thing was that he couldn't actually read the time. To overcome this difficulty, he used to look at his watch vaguely and say, "You'd never think it was that time," hoping that the person he was talking to would look at their own watch and say, "Oh, it's a quarter to eleven. I'd better go." He'd always get the time that way – then the job was oxo [simple to do].

One morning, Georgie called to a neighbour of ours to do a thatching job and, since it was still early, he took leave to wash his teeth under the big pump in the yard. The oul' farmer never saw anybody washing teeth or doing anything like that because he was reared up not washing them.

"Jaysus," he cried in surprise, gazing toothless out at the thatcher from the half door. "Would some of ye come quick because George Bannon is frothing at the mouth!"

Georgie was a character and although he had a thing for me, it never came to anything despite oul' Posie's best efforts to make a match. In the end he did get married, but already had a large family to bring to the wedding. The priest was bemused by the sight of all the children sitting in the chapel and decided he would enquire about it before the ceremony.

"Well Father," Georgie whispered reverently, "four of them are mine and the other five are hers!"

CHAPTER TWELVE

The Buttermilk and the Hat

After Sunday Mass, my father went to the hut and took out a couple of scythes. When he was satisfied that they were sharp enough, he unchained the bogie and, together with the lads, went down the line to cut hay. During the summer it was a common sight to see railway gangs out on the line, cutting the grass and overgrowth away from the sides of the track. Like the men in his gang, my father didn't work on Sunday, but if his services were ever required, the rate for all grades except watchmen and crossing keepers was time and a quarter.

On this occasion, the day was free for the cutting of grass and he made long low swishes, deepening his rhythm as he cut away from the embankment. Although the scythe was a dangerous implement, he had experience in using one and with help from the lads, was soon finished. Instructing them to load up the bogie, he contented himself with the fact that there was enough fodder to last the animals another while.

Before coming home, Joe had gone into a huxtery shop called Phelan's that sold nothing but the best of sweets and, as usual, he brought a huge bag home to my mother. When I opened the little gate and came into the kitchen, she had the breakfast on. I had hitched a lift home from Mass in a neighbour's pony and trap and looked forward to a big piece of bacon or beef out of the pan. I was also hoping for a few sweets and could also count on my mother for those, but this morning she was too engrossed in setting the table to notice that I had come in. At the fire, the boiling pot of potatoes bristled with steam, sending hot spatters of water onto the hearth. 'Them spuds'll go into prowsh [mush],' she muttered as she hobbled over to take them off the boil.

I knew that the bag of sweets was deep down in one of my mother's apron pockets, so I tiptoed up behind her. So long as I was careful, I was able to lift away to my heart's content. I had a master feed of gobstoppers and hard boilers but eventually she put a hand in to find them almost gone.

"Ah, I'm left with a whole load of *feck* nothin'," she cried, throwing her arms into the air. "You're getting n'more of them, the next time Joe brings them," she cautioned.

That afternoon – his work done – my father packed his timber reel, his traces and his bait and lifted the fishing rod onto his shoulder.

"A master day for it," he said – gazing out the window at the overcast sky. Like most fishermen, he swore that a cloudy day with a breeze on the water was good for bringing up the fish.

With the dog yapping at his heels, he trudged across the fields to a spot on the Brosna called the Monastery River. There, he met his two fishing friends – Jim Rafter, who was an insurance agent and Pat Rabbitte from Kilcoursey. Pat, who was slightly deaf, arrived as usual with the fishing traces sticking out of his collar. Once, when he was crossing the field with rod in hand, a neighbour shouted, "Are you goin' fishing, Pat?"

"Ah no," replied the bothered fisherman, "I'm goin' fishing!"

Arriving at the riverbank, my father assembled his wooden rod patiently. For bait, he used frogs from the Mill Pond, the legs of which he tied with velvet ribbon. He claimed that the colour attracted the fish. When all was ready, he swung his line over the peaty waters and sat down to wait.

After he had gone, my mother muttered as she poked around

the hearth.

"Nothing good will come from that oul' fishing – staring into nothing only water. He'll take a lightness now, so he will. Then he'll waltz."

As she shuffled outside to take some water from the barrel, she could still be heard muttering to herself: "A lightness; that's what he'll get now for his trouble." She had that idea in her head, because she believed that if my father waited too long for a bite, his eyes might be entranced by the running waters of the Brosna.

The previous week, he had moved down to Charlestown where he caught a couple of eels under the dark churning waters of the bridge. Once the heads and tails had been cut off, they were hung in the kitchen where, after a while, they began to curl up like hooks.

At six o'clock that evening, my mother's niece, Mary Burke, arrived with great punctuality from Aughamore. Like her relations in Kilmucklin, she was very proper and ladylike, so when I found out that she was coming I made plans to get out of her way. As I was closing the gate on my way to the Sacred Heart Sodality, she came up behind me.

"Going to meet the boys?" she said in her usual starchy manner. Startled, I turned and scurried up the lane with my bicycle.

In those days, we learned to cycle almost before we learned to walk, and I covered the miles into Clara easily. My bike had been bought from Kenny's for £3 fifty on hire purchase and my father, who warned me to look after it, showed me how to look out for the tell-tale sign of 'duck-eggs' – bulges in the inner tube when the tyre was growing thin.

The Sodality was held once a month at seven o'clock and involved the saying of the Rosary followed by a Mass. All the members lined up in their own pew, which had a banner standing in a metal pole ring near the aisle. That was used when the procession came through the town. Fortunately however, it was usually over before eight o'clock, and since all the young people were forced to go, it was a great place to make a date. Sometimes I arranged to meet a lad halfway and didn't go at all!

But when I came out, I saw with dismay that all the bikes were pegged out of the way. My cousin Minnie Burke, who had arrived at the Sodality after me, had lumped hers on top of mine. She was an awful nuisance, wore strange clothes and bought holy pictures when the Mission came to town, but since my father was courting favour with my Aunt Delia for the land around Kilmucklin, he forced me to go with her. I couldn't get away this time either because my bike – a man's version with a crossbar – stood out from all the others.

When I eventually managed to give her the slip, I headed for the big beech tree at the top of the road. Many of the farmer's sons had lined up there on Doorley's wall, because Sunday was a big recreation day for them. The top of the lane was a favourite place to play cards, hurling and football but the most popular game by far was pitch and toss. The players got their chance to aim a coin closest to a stone in the middle of the road. Known locally as the 'Spud', the player who got closest to it became the 'Tosser'. That meant that he called the toss, betting that out of four throws, his coin would land either twice on heads or on harps.

The old penny was prized, because it had a good weight for throwing and there were a few shillings to be won. A large crowd had gathered around the key players, but with all the shuffling feet, so much dust rose that the men couldn't see where they had thrown their coin.

When it got too dark to play, the pitch and toss school wound its way down to our house, and my father read the newspaper aloud to them. Soon a debate started – a sign that it was time for a smoke. As the men rambled on they withdrew clay pipes from their pockets and began to clean them, scraping dried tobacco from the bowls and tapping the residue into the grate. My father's pipe was no ordinary clay instrument, but was made from wood and had a crooked stem. While he listened intently to the argument, he took down some plug tobacco, cut it with a knife and softened the pieces between his thumb and index finger. Then he struck a match, put it to his pipe and stuck his own oar in.

I laughed at the ramblers because they were like old men to me, blinding everyone with smoke and talking nonsense. They were all dressed up with shiny boots, starched Sunday shirts and smart hats, which, even with the heat from the hearth they never took off. It was this final detail that gave me a great brainwave to do some divilment.

I thought of the woman in the shop in Clara, who made her sweet bags by turning a piece of paper around in a cone and twisting a little knob at the bottom of it. For a long time I sat on the settle bed in the kitchen, listening to the debate and wondered where I could get a bag like that. Eventually, I remembered where my mother kept some brown paper that had been used to wrap the meat from town. I jumped off the settle bed, ran to the dresser and reached in behind the jugs. When I had cut and wound the paper the way they did it in the shop, I slipped into the parlour room and, standing on tiptoe, filled my own little bag with buttermilk from the big churn.

Out in the kitchen meanwhile, the argument was beginning to heat up. One side of the floor was taking my father's side, but a man from Doury was getting support from another neighbour who had just walked in. Both sides were engrossed in the argument but nobody minded that I was there. As quiet as a mouse, I walked around behind them all.

My father was the chairman, telling the height of lies and yarns by the score. As I crept behind the ramblers I whispered, 'Eeny meeny miney moe, catch a piggy by the toe.' The man I chose was wearing a lovely suit that was sure to be put up until next Sunday, so I walked around behind him and emptied out my little bag. It was very serious talk and the buttermilk nearly got churned in the crease of his hat.

CHAPTER THIRTEEN

Tyre tracks on the Bog Road

Doctor O'Hara, who was a tall, distinguished looking man, was in the habit of parking at our house. He never drove down the bog road because, although the surface suited the hooves of donkeys as they made their way out to Doury Bog, it was certain to destroy the delicate tyres of a motor vehicle. Armed instead with a carpetbag full of medicine, he would walk the half-mile or so down to Wogan's, where there were always children being born. We pronounced the name as 'Ugan' so if anyone called to the railway house looking for them, it would be like looking for a needle in a sack of straw.

Despite his skill as a physician, the doctor had a very abrupt manner. Once, while coming out of his surgery in Church Street in Clara, he was stopped by an old woman who had come to town to do her shopping. Since it was a windy day, she said by way of conversation, "I was near being blown away," to which he blithely snapped: "It'd be no loss!"

She wasn't long getting her own back, because when O'Hara and some friends were playing golf one day, she happened to be walking past the course. What could she shout only: "Did you find yer hole, Doctor?"

In those days, there were few cars and we recognised the deep tread left by O'Hara's wheels. When we were very young however, tyre tracks on a boreen or the hum of engines often meant something different.

One cold December morning, we were all getting ready to set out for Mass and we waited while my father took our russet-coloured pony into the yard and harnessed him to the trap. This took a while, since the remembrance of an old incident at the laneway gate always made him buck and fret.

When my father had finished, he whistled to us to come out and opened the trap at the back. It had room for four people – two facing two. Heavy springs underneath helped to cushion us from potholes on the main road, but there was little protection from the weather. I was helped up because I was too small to climb the metal step and I sat alongside my mother. When the pony was harnessed properly, we were given a blanket to keep out the cold and we trotted towards the main road.

As we neared the junction, the pony cocked its ears and snorted nervously into the cold air. A few moments later, we discovered for ourselves what had startled the animal. In the distance, the sound of motor engines approached and in the next instant, a convoy of trucks rattled by, full of soldiers in khaki-coloured uniforms. They were returning to their barracks in Tullamore.

My father drew up the reins to stop the trap until the soldiers had passed. Meanwhile, I sat wide-eyed and amazed, as if it was a circus going by. It seemed to take forever and clouds of dust rose off the dirt road.

Suddenly our pony took fright at the unfamiliar noise of engines and began to shy. If it bolted, there was a danger that the trap could turn over but fortunately, a young officer recognised the danger and ordered the truck to halt. He leapt down and barked to two privates standing behind him. "Stop that animal," he shouted, motioning in our direction. Obeying this order, the soldiers ran to where we sat, grabbed the pony's harness and eventually succeeded in calming him.

The officer, who wore a brass-buttoned greatcoat, strode over to apologise to my father and doffed his cap to my mother.

"Are you alright ma'm?" he asked.

"I'm grand *a Mhuirnín*," she replied, not knowing what to make of it all.

"I rather expect that your pony would have made a dash for it," the officer laughed.

He was a thorough gentleman. I thought it was great excitement, because, being small I didn't understand the danger. Afterwards, I discovered that this was the day that the Treaty was being signed.

Besides the presence of British soldiers, we also had direct experience of the Volunteers who depended on locals for help, particularly if they were to win the war.

One night, my father heard the sound of bicycles in the lane and went to the door. He found a group of young lads standing there, some of whom he recognised as neighbours' sons and friends of my brother Joe. Stepping forward, the leader hailed him and asked for the key of the railway hut.

After checking that the coast was clear, the lads set off in twos, walking down the line to borrow picks and hacks. One of them stayed with the bicycles to keep watch in case of trouble. This was understandable, since we were under martial law and unless you were a police constable or soldier, you weren't supposed to be cycling anywhere.

When the rest of the gang returned, they all walked to the top of the lane. Under cover of darkness, they stood out on the main road and dug holes in it like boyos. The aim of course was to prevent easy movement for British soldiers. The first trench was huge – almost as large as a shell hole, but they left a narrow causeway for foot traffic and of course for bicycles.

Finally, tired and dirty, they streamed back down the lane and returned the tools to the shed. Before collecting their bicycles, they came inside to chat to my father and mother. In the kitchen, there was a wardrobe that my grandfather had made and several of them admired it. As they sat around, eating the last of my mother's bread, I took in their general appearance. Scruffy from the dirt of the road, the leader wore jodhpurs, which were leather boots like riding breeches. Some of the other lads wore 'puttees'; a yard and a half of cloth, starting on the ankles and wound up to the knees to distinguish them as Volunteers. After draining the dregs of tea from their mugs, they returned the key to my father, thanked my mother and went to the gate. Climbing the stile with their bikes, they slipped home across Doury bog.

That night, I could hear my parents speaking. They slept above the kitchen to the left of the hearth, whereas I shared a room with my sisters Bab and Ciss, next to the yard. My father had wound the bedstead springs tight that morning and grateful for the removal of any creaks, I scrambled over the jute sack blanket and pressed my ear to the wall.

"Nothing good'll come from the like of that baileabhairing," my mother was saying.

"Arra whist, woman,' my father replied. "Sure don't they have to do something."

"The Lord save us," my mother retorted. "And sure wasn't my own poor grandmother doing something long 'go, when them all was starving, and she getting them to kneel and say the Rosary before a feed of stirabout, but she never done anything to bring trouble home. May the Lord save us and keep us."

The next morning, my mother's fears were borne out. As she busied herself at the hearth, the silence was pierced by the distant hum of engines.

"My Jesus here they are!" she cried as she dropped the hot griddle and ran to the bedroom window to see what was happening.

Full of curiosity, I got down from the kitchen stool and jumped up on the bed behind her.

The sound grew closer and closer until suddenly, through the dusty windowpane, we could see a vehicle covered in steel netting lurching down the laneway. It was a Crossley tender with three Black and Tans inside.

"*Oh Mhuire, Mhuire,*" my mother cried as she blessed herself in fear.

After what seemed like forever, the Crossley came to a halt outside the railway house. One of the soldiers marched up the stone path and rapped heavily on the door. Finding no answer, he walked straight into the kitchen. My mother ran out of the bedroom and stood in front of the table, where Joe and Tommie were sitting eating stirabout.

"Move aside," the soldier barked gruffly.

You never knew exactly what the Black and Tans would do when they came to your house. Sometimes they might break things or take valuables, and once they went into a poor neighbour of ours and stole all his food.

Fortunately for us, this soldier was more concerned with filling the holes than he was with filling his pockets.

"Come on," he shouted. "Get out and bring your shovels to fill in that."

He waited while Joe scrambled down the line to fetch some shovels from the shed. Then, taking Tommie by the scruff of the neck, he frogmarched him up the lane. Tommie and Joe were barely able to carry a shovel, let alone use one. As they walked, they were joined by other neighbours who had been forced from their homes. If they hadn't got shovels, they were supplied.

Meanwhile, my mother knelt down on the stone flag and said a Hail Mary to Our Lady to prevent her sons from doing anything to upset the English soldiers.

"Jesus, send them back to me," she prayed.

The Black and Tans were capable of shooting them like dogs if they resisted, so we felt lucky to see them coming back at all.

That evening, my father, who was furious, paced angrily in front of the fire before storming out the back door. When he returned, he thumbed through the calendar to find an oft-quoted passage written on a scrap of paper. His voice shaking with temper, he spat:

*'That the providence of God,
Which sometimes here,
Afflicts the good and prospers the bad,
May appear before all men someday.'*

My poor mother, who said nothing, was just thankful that nothing more serious had befallen her beloved sons.

CHAPTER FOURTEEN

Trip to the Well

One evening, after my mother had finished milking our two cows, she took the heavy tin pails into the kitchen and set them down on the stone floor. First, she put the milk into wide pans and when the cream came to the surface, she skimmed it off.

Over a few days, this cream was gradually collected and stored in a couple of brown-coloured crocks that we kept in one of the sheds. The crocks were left to sit until the cream in them had gone a little bit sour. When that happened, my mother sat the barrel churn on the kitchen table and began to make butter. As her plump arms worked, she sang like the music hall singer Florrie Forde, in step with the turning handle:

Come, come, come and make eyes at me,
Down at the old Bull and Bush.

When a neighbour called during the churning, he didn't turn his back on it. With a hearty cry of 'God bless the work,' he took the handle and gave it a couple of turns for luck. There was a glass window in the churn and when that was getting clear we knew the butter was nearly ready. Eventually the buttermilk was drained off and then it was time to take out all the beaters.

When we looked in, the churn was full of butter. Scooping it out, my mother began to make big pounds on a dish using a wooden pattie for the shape. The top of the milk was very greasy so the crock would have to be scalded with boiling water and that meant a trip to the well.

In those days, nearly every family kept a rainwater barrel at the corner of the house for washing clothes and potatoes, but the water was no good for drinking. For that, we had to go to a spring well nearby.

An old family called Robbins lived at the corner of the lane where we turned with our buckets. They kept cows and Ellen, like my mother, made butter from the milk. Putting it into a basket, she made the regular journey into D.E. Williams' shop in Clara to sell it and when you smelled it, you knew it was real country butter.

Ellen also had a brother called Ned who often rambled up to our house. We used to have great skit with him too, because he nearly always had a hole in the back of his trousers. My God, half the shirt would be pulled out with us because we'd all get a go at it! He'd be hitting the ground with his foot telling my father something, but when he turned around we'd have the shirt almost pulled off him.

As we passed the Robbins' house, the half door was open as usual, so we went in for skit. Inside, the floor hadn't been swept for weeks. Ellen, who was dirty and wrinkle-faced, had nothing but a few plates on the dresser, and pecking around the floor were chickens of various breeds. One of them scratched around the boxty bread cooking on the griddle, before picking off a square and running outside with it.

The fire was going on a hearth full of ashes and a teapot sat in the middle of it instead of hanging on the crane. When Ellen saw us at the door, she hooshed the remaining chickens out with her apron and offered us what was left of the bread. It looked as though she hadn't washed for a month, but she lived to be nearly a hundred despite what they tell you about hygiene.

The floor was so dirty that you could write your name on it, which gave Larry an idea. When Ellen wasn't looking, he stooped down and wrote some words in the ashes near the hearth. The words, which sounded like the name of a horse, read 'Hoof Hearted. Ice melted'. It sounded cruel but she didn't know what he was doing. Before she had time to turn around, we ran out the door laughing, swinging our pails and didn't stop until we got to the end of the road.

At the well, spring water gushed over mosses and lichen and it was all the time flowing, even in the dry days of summer. Carefully, we climbed down the steps, lowered our pails and filled them until they were as heavy as we could manage. Ellen, meanwhile, never went down any steps. To get water, she used to go over the road and stick an oul' kettle or pot into the drain with branches growing out of it. Considering where she got the water to make the tea with, it's a wonder that she lived to be such a great age.

Although we used a lot of water, we managed without a pump for a long time. After a few years however, the older lads were able to sink a well by divining for water themselves using a hazel rod. They all trailed along to the front of the house until the rod began to point downwards and that was where they dug. A pump cylinder, consisting of many joined pipes was placed into the ground until it eventually reached the water table. This connected to an above-ground handle and spout housing which my father painted red. A sucker rod then went into the cylinder, making a kind of piston to pump the water with. A granite basin was placed underneath to catch the fresh water. It took a few goes to gradually force the water from the bottom of the well to the spout and into the bucket, but it worked. It was fantastic because we hadn't to go for water then.

When news got around that the Gaynors had a pump, all the neighbours started to arrive with buckets. Norah Bergin, the daughter of Oul' Tim, was one of the first. She came down from the top of the lane one day to get a bucket of water, and was greeted by none other than my cousin Jody Spollen. Jody's mother was my father's sister who married the Tailor Spollen of Daingean.

Before his bike accident, Uncle Tom used to sit up on the table with his brother Bernie, and they stitched away with their legs crossed in concentration. Sometimes they came down to our house to make suits for the lads. 'I'll have that for you next week' was the usual answer to any question regarding the finished article, but they might as well be idle. They were the greatest liars who ever lived, but they were great tailors.

Like his father, Jody was an awful jeer and Norah was anything but good looking. As she was pumping away, he turned around to take a good look at her.

"My God," he exclaimed, "You shouldn't be drawing oul' water and feeding pigs. Sure you're only fit for breaking boys' hearts."

She was delighted with herself. Well, I laughed to myself, you fecking oul' jeer you. Thinking that she had been paid a compliment, Norah blushed and went on filling her bucket. When she had finished, she offered it to Jody.

"Would you have a sup of water sir?" she asked.

He looked at her in a funny way and exclaimed "Nobody says 'Sir' but a tinker!"

CHAPTER FIFTEEN

Holidays in Dublin

On the morning of his departure for Dublin, my father sharpened his razor on a piece of leather and poised himself at the kitchen table. The blade was an open one and he had to have a very steady hand for the job. When he was ready, my mother lifted the small swing-mirror from its place on the windowsill and placed it carefully in front of him. With his braces hanging down around his trousers, he slowly ran the blade over his face, returning it to the enamel basin every so often. When he had finished, he used some of the leftover soap to curl his moustache into a point at both ends.

Satisfied with the outcome, he whistled off into the bedroom to put on the new suit that he had ordered from Tom Spollen. The trousers were button fly and there was a waistcoat and jacket to match. It had cost him twenty-one shillings – the equivalent of over a week's wages.

The fifteenth of August had arrived and we were preparing to spend a week with my Uncle Joe and Aunt Nanny in Inchicore. My mother, for her part, set about dressing me as nicely as she could for the train journey.

"Now Tom, don't have her out visiting anywhere without her hair done right. Nanny'll be able to do that for ye," she advised as she ran a brush through my dark hair. "And you make sure and have manners *a Lana*," she reminded, taking my two hands in her own.

Soon it was time for breakfast and she swung the kettle out on the crane and lifted it off gingerly with a cloth. She poured some tea for my father and served us both a breakfast of rashers and sausages.

Later on, Joe drove us into Clara in the pony and trap, and we parked in the little yard beside the station. During the winter, the haltkeeper always kept the fire lit in the reception room for the benefit of passengers but during the summer it was more comfortable and less smoky to sit on the platform benches. Outside, the sun had not yet fallen onto the station building and the three tall gas lamps stood in shade. On the walls, advertisements for 'Tyler's Boots' fought for space with 'Suttons Seeds'. An air of quiet expectancy had fallen over the platform, broken only by the occasional sound of garden birds.

As he stood waiting, my father watched as a drab-looking train made ready for its journey down the Banagher line. The line, which ran as far as the Shannon, had been worked by Joe Gaynor and by almost every other railwayman out of Inchicore. At home, my father once said to my mother that the orders Joe got from Kingsbridge that time were like Cromwell's. With that in mind, he gazed intently towards the hut as the driver of the paint-peeling engine handed the staff to the lineman. 'To Hell or to Banagher,' he murmured.

Soon, our own train pulled in, hissing steam. The station porter arrived to open the doors with a cry of 'All aboard!' My father helped me up the step into the oil-lit carriage and when we found our seats, he took off his bowler hat and smoothed back his hair. After the train had finished taking on water, he smiled broadly, gripped my hand and the carriage heaved into life.

As we passed the railway crossing, I stood on the seat and waved excitedly to my mother who was standing at our front door fluttering a white handkerchief – the same way she did for Ciss each time she left for Dublin.

After changing trains in Kildare, the last stop was Kingsbridge and the station was full of noise and smoke from engines coming in and out. I thought it was shocking big compared to Clara station at home, and I looked forward to getting a jaunt on the trams. I wanted to see everything at once. But then my father put a hand on my shoulder.

"Easy now Cat," he said gently. "I know ye're all excited, but don't forget that we have to get to Aunt Nanny's house first."

Taking me by the hand, he led me out to where all the jarveys stood with their horses.

We soon found a man willing to take us to Inchicore. My father helped me into the trap and then sat in beside me. Soon we were passing Kilmainham Gaol and the large red brick houses of Inchicore road. Clipping past the model school and Cleary's public house, the jarvey quickened his pace as the trap moved between the high grey walls of the railway embankment. As we passed underneath the bridge, the *scallop* of the horse's hooves echoed around us. Finally, with a switch of the reins, the driver passed the Khyber Pass, a narrow laneway used by the railwaymen to get to the works.

Aunt Nanny lived in Albion Terrace near the 'Ranch' – a small railway community made up of First Avenue, Liffey Street, Park Street, Phoenix Street, St Mary's Avenue and St Mary's Terrace. A lot of railway people lived there on account of Inchicore GS&WR works being nearby, and most of the families had some connection with the railway. Of these, most were fitters and boiler men. Besides this class of workers, engine drivers and firemen also found lodgings in the Ranch when they were staying in Dublin.

Nanny was a big fat woman and there was always plenty of food at her house. She was delighted to see me and soon after we arrived, she dressed me in lovely short stockings and a little turn-down top with new shoes and buckles to match. I was delighted with myself and showed them off, since you might say she dressed me from top to bottom. For the whole holiday I was to sleep in a huge big bed in a little room off the parlour. I was a favourite of my father's brother Joe, who, upon arriving home from Guinness's brewery, codded with me as if I were one of his own.

Many of the houses in the Ranch were single-storey, with one hall door and two rooms either side of a long hallway. In First Avenue, the people kept allotments where they grew their own vegetables and fruit. They kept goats and horses and there were some families who reared pigs: it really was like being in the country. Like us at home, the children who lived there were used to the railway and could tell the time by the sound of passing goods and passenger trains.

Also living in Inchicore with his wife was an older cousin of mine called Joe Doherty. His mother, Aunt Mary still lived in Clashawaun in a little row of houses. A tall man would nearly have to turn a cripple to go in. I often visited her for no other reason but to get some lovely apple tart or a cake, because Aunt Mary was a great cook.

Joe used to come down on the train to visit his mother but was never any length there when he'd come out to Ashfield to see us. I used to love to see him coming down to the railway house because he always gave me a pound in return for a kiss. When he was gone, all the lads would gather around and cod me.

"That one's after kissing that oul' egit," they would sneer, so I used to shake the money in my fist and shout, "You know what I'm going to tell you? I'd kiss his arse if he gave me another pound!"

One morning, as we sat having breakfast with Aunt Nanny, my father put his knife and fork down and looked at me intently.

"I was thinking of taking you for a jaunt as far as Kingstown to see Ciss," he said with twinkling eyes. "But you better be on your best behaviour for me now, do you hear?"

I nodded excitedly. When we were ready, we left the house and took the Number 21 tram into town from its terminus at the Black Lion pub. At College Green, he paid the two pence fare to the conductor and we walked across the bridge towards Nelson's pillar.

I wondered at all the cars parked on the island in the middle, because there was nothing like that in the country. On the bridge, a Jewman with a camera took our 'sticky-back' and my father paid with a promise to get it posted to Ashfield. Then he took my hand and we crossed the busy road, past the white-gloved policeman directing traffic at the junction.

As he stood at the counter of Kapp and Peterson's buying plug tobacco for his pipe, I marvelled at all the blue and crème-coloured trams waiting to take passengers on to the suburbs or to the seaside. Nelson was alive and kicking and the pillar was the head place for everyone to meet, especially for people coming from the country. Everywhere, you could hear people saying, 'I'll meet you at Nelson's Pillar.' Amidst the flower sellers and parked trams, they shook hands, went shopping and made a day of it in Dublin.

Nelson's Pillar was also the Terminus — when the Dalkey tram was set for the return journey, the conductor made ready to face it in the right direction. First, he dismounted and, by means of a long pole, pulled the overhead trolley into the correct position. After that, he only had to run his hand across the seats so that they faced the driver. For some reason my seat hadn't been turned so I sat down and faced all the other passengers.

When I stared at them, they stared back. 'What the God damn is it,' I wondered. 'Why are they all sitting looking at me?' I couldn't understand why I was sitting in that position and no one had bothered to tell me — not even my father, who was chatting to the driver downstairs. But I was up in Dublin and had to let on I knew it all.

How small I got when we reached Merrion Square and I realised my dilemma.

It reminds me of a yarn I often heard told about the trams. Two men came up from the country on a holiday and made straight for O'Connell Bridge. One of them looked and saw a parked tram with an advertisement for Bovril along its side and a sign for the Zoo on the front, so he turned to the other fella and scratched his head. "Will we go to Bovril now?" he asked. "Or will we go to the Zoo?" The other oul' lad didn't know what to say, because he didn't know where Bovril was.

The journey to Kingstown was long but very exciting and soon, the tram was rattling into George's Street, with its busy shops and daytime strollers. Pulling back the scissors cage, my father helped me down the step and with a friendly wave parted company with the driver. Then we made our way directly to the Royal Marine Hotel near the pier.

"We'll get our dinner out," winked my father, "because the bigger the hotel, the bigger the price."

As we came through the wide entrance, he removed his bowler hat and smoothed back his hair. Waiting while he enquired after Ciss at the reception desk, I glanced with wide eyes at the grand lobby and its white marble floor. Through a set of double doors was a lounge filled with tables and an old piano. In front of us, a wide staircase led up to a sunlit landing from which two other staircases branched to the right and left.

A few minutes later Ciss swept down the stairs like some kind of film star – her hair a mass of curls and her face beaming with delight.

"Well, what do ye think of my engagement ring?" she squealed, holding out her hand.

"You just better be careful," my father said warily, opening his arms wide. "Your Aunt Katie knows the lad from Kilkenny and he likes his drink."

"Arra would you go 'way," Ciss replied. "Sure I'll be grand."

My father doted on his eldest daughter, and always introduced her proudly as such when she was home on holiday. He didn't want to see her getting into trouble.

We strolled across the road and towards the pier until we came across a group of milesmen digging on the railway with shovels. "God bless the work," my father said cheerfully. While on holiday, he always took an interest in men who were involved in the same profession as himself. Salty and hardy-faced, the Kingstown gang looked more like sailors than milesmen, and as they talked, they puffed loudly on their pipes and laughed heartily.

When we eventually reached the end of the pier, I sat on a crate and looked around. Alongside us, fishermen's nets bleached and toughened in the sun. My father reclined on a hawser and took out his pipe. Summoning a match to his hand, he placed it over the bowl and the sweet, almond aroma of Mick McQuaid Plug drifted into the summer sky.

Docked at the far pier, the funnel of a mail boat steamed lazily and he watched it for a long time without speaking.

"Well, ye're in the right place," he said eventually. "A job that's real clean and proper and the sea beside ye. I suppose you could do worse than here and go t'England. Then what would I do for a holiday?"

To me, Ciss seemed terribly grown up and might as well have been living in America as far as I was concerned.

Afterwards, as my father and sister returned along the pier, I ran up and down the steps of the sea wall and played at being 'Dublin' for a while, letting on that I was really sophisticated. Ciss eventually noticed my antics and took a fit of laughing. The previous month, a local woman, returning from a two-week holiday in the city, had interrupted my mother from laying the tablecloth with: "Oh Mrs Gaynor, don't go to any trouble on my account. I never changed."

Meanwhile, seagulls whirled noisily overhead, squabbling and diving towards the green-coloured water. I was dying to play on the steps again but my father had an edge on him from the sea air, so we walked briskly up to George's Street where we took a table near the window in the Kingstown Coffee Palace. A large steaming pot of tea arrived and we ordered buns and scones.

"I'm away to the Abbey tonight," my father enthused, "And I'll prob'ly get on for a drink afterwards in Clery's, so I'd better get this little one back to Inchicore."

My sister gave me a funny look to make me laugh since she knew that her father was sure to drink wherever there was porter.

"How's Mam?" she asked.

"Oh, the Doctor come out from Clonshanny," I cried, dying to tell the story. "He walked up and down in his plus fours and didn't know what to be giving her. All he said was 'that sounds like a hive of bees'."

Ciss and my father laughed at that. It was good to see them in such good humour. My mother's recent bout of asthma had been so bad that Ciss was summoned by wire to say her last goodbyes.

Later, as we crossed the lengthening shadows of the street and into the gardens of the Royal Marine, my father reassured her.

"Make sure and say your prayers and your Rosary," he said. "There's a good girl."

Then, pressing some money into her hand near the bandstand, he watched her walk into the lobby and out of sight.

It was Wednesday morning when we returned to Clara and the station was busy with the sounds and smells of cattle being loaded for the Dublin Cattle Market. As the frightened animals were driven into the waiting wagons, occasionally one would try to jump the gate – much to the annoyance of the men herding them.

While we waited at a safe distance for Joe to arrive with the pony and trap, one of the drovers spotted my father with his new suit and blackthorn stick. Calling over the bellowing, snuffling throng, he shouted: "Hey, how are things in the Dáil, Tom?"

CHAPTER SIXTEEN

Autumn Divilment

When autumn came, my mother arranged the oats money, whereas my father – preferring to leave such church affairs alone – went to help his neighbours with their harvest. On the day of the threshing he joined a gang of men in the yard, and waited with them as the big paraffin-fuelled machine rolled into the haggard to thresh the corn and the wheat. The grain collected into bags at the mouth of the thresher. At the back, amidst the great noise, the men were kept busy collecting the discarded straw into big stacks.

According to the part of the townsland in which they were situated, the stacks of straw or hay were either called 'cocks' or 'trams'. When formed into a tram, the hay was straddled by a rope to flatten it down, and bricks were placed on either side to secure it. Roping it was a two-man job. The first man would wait on a ladder for the second to throw a *súgán* from the other side. As they worked, they wore a hay cover on the caps of their knees which helped to keep the frost away and when they came in and out of our house, you'd get a grassy smell from them. It was straw and hay that kept them alive.

One day, Larry and I noticed that the rope on a tram in the field where we were playing had great pull, due to the careful placement of two large blocks on either side. Like mountain climbers, we gave the rope a couple of cautious tugs and when we were satisfied that it would hold our weight, we raced each other to the top.

We had great gas then and knocked down every bit of the stack by dancing on it.

Entirely taken up by our efforts, neither of us noticed our father, who was on his way home from work. When his bike rounded the bend, his mouth fell open as he took in the state we had left the tram of hay. In a panic, we slithered down the rope, ran into the house and dived under the bed.

A few seconds later, he stormed into the kitchen.

"Where are they?" he bellowed.

"Where's who?" my mother replied, because she didn't know what we had done.

"Where are they?" he shouted again. "I'll kill them."

We wouldn't move when we heard my father say that and couldn't be found then. Now we were lost.

Since it was autumn, the evening drew in early and soon it was dark. Needless to say, my parents got no dinner and had neighbours out looking for us. For several miles, their lanterns swung – along the track, up the laneway and over Doury bog. Meanwhile we were beginning to enjoy ourselves under the bed. We lay quiet as mice amongst the shoes and empty suitcases, playing with marbles on the stone floor and hoping that nobody would hear us.

We were having a ball until the door suddenly opened. From our hiding place, we could see the dusty trousers of a workman striding towards the bed and the springs creaked heavily as he sat down.

"Where the hell would they be now?" my father enquired from the kitchen.

"Ah sure, wouldn't you know they run when they saw you coming from the field," the man replied.

From our position, we could see that the workman was wearing an oul' pair of shoes full of holes. In the rain, they would certainly let in water so he had come in to fetch a better pair that might suit the muck of the road. We used to call these boots 'cattle wagons', because that's what they would remind you of – two feet, one shunting in front of the other like two railway cars.

As he reached down to fish for a pair of boots, he heard our scuffling as we tried to move further back. With that, his grisly old head peered down under the bed and he exclaimed, "The Lord save us! Here they are, Mr Gaynor!"

When my mother and father heard that, they came running, and in their relief at finding us under the bed instead of in a drain, they forgot about all the mischief we had caused.

One dark cold night soon afterwards, Aunt Katie arrived from Bagenalstown. Since she was to stay for the night, I was told to sleep in the parlour room.

I made a face because the parlour was like a barracks – cold in winter and difficult to heat because the fireplace was very small. The biggest piece of furniture in it was an old press bed onto which my father had glued little carved garlands and flowers. It looked like a press standing upright until he opened it out into a bed for me to sleep in. Over this, he laid a blanket made from empty flour bags sewn together.

After tea, Aunt Katie sat at the fire and chatted with my mother. Meanwhile, my father, who wanted to keep well out of it, put on his glasses and lit the reading lamp to study the newspaper. None of them stirred, and it seemed as though everyone but Larry and I were content with what they were doing.

The room was very warm because Joe's fireman's coat was tucked in under the doorjamb. Noticing it after a long interval, my mother put her hands to her face and exclaimed, "The Lord save us! Who put Joe's good pilot coat there at the door?"

"Ah," my father said, peering over the top of his newspaper to give me the eye, "don't you know who did that?"

Eventually, the coat was hung back behind the door and something else was found for the draught.

All that talk gave both Lar and I a brainwave.

"We'll friken me father with this thing," I giggled, waving one coat arm daringly. "But we need something to make it stan' up."

As quiet as mice, we went out into the yard and found the handle of a brush. Then we sneaked the pilot coat out, put it on the brush handle with a hat on top and laid it against the back door.

We knew that my father would soon open the door to relieve himself at the pit – a place near the sheds full of cow dung and other rubbish that, when full, was used as fertiliser for growing vegetables. When he opened the door, the big 'man' that we had made was sure to fall on top of him.

Satisfied that everything was ready, we came inside to observe my father's movements. After a while, he started to get a bit agitated and made for the back door. As we watched, he opened it, shut it quickly, and went the colour of whitewash. Larry and I looked at each another and smiled broadly, since it was obvious that he had been frightened out of his wits. He walked around the house whistling and taking quick glances towards the door. His mind must have raced with visions of every banshee and pooka that he had ever heard of, but after a while, he summoned up the courage to go outside again. With the fright he got when the coat fell on top of him, I think he must still be jumping.

If we weren't out to entertain our parents, we were being entertained ourselves. As the crowd gathered at the fire on a cold winter's night, the stories would start. The storyteller might tell some lies, but full of the joys of spring, he always had a good gift of the gab and held our attention. Often, for our amusement, he would tell a riddle, the answer to which we guessed in vain. One of these ran as follows:

What has long legs, short thighs,
Little head and no eyes?

"See if ye can get him now," the rambler would say encouragingly. The answer was of course staring us in the face. Resting by the hearth, it was none other than the long tongs. At other times, no hard thinking was needed and we simply sat and listened to the storyteller's yarns. As the night drew in, these came thick and fast and as we listened, our eyes grew as wide as cartwheels.

When a few local lads were looking for divilment they would put a stick up with a white cloak on it at a crossroads. The road out of Clara was winding and lonely at night and if you were going along on the bicycle and looked sideways at the sheet blowing in the wind, you might think it was a ghost.

As the days grew even shorter, we also used to go across the bog to Doury wood to gather nuts and cherries. What a quiet place it was. You could be dead for months and no one would ever get you. Although we were too nervous to play there very often, the wood was a great place for gathering hazel scallops to hold down the thatch and for the hazelnuts that grew in abundance. We'd come along and shake them from the trees. When we got them home, we used one of my father's tools to get at the kernel or 'kurnel' as we called them. At that time of year, we also looked into the ditches for blackberries, which started out red before bruising under the sun to a darker colour. If we couldn't find enough of these, we sometimes looked for cherry trees.

Some mornings, we rose early and went into the fields to pick mushrooms. The mushrooms were small, like buttons, but amongst those were others that we had to watch out for. These were poisonous and if you ate one it would make you very sick.

When we returned to the railway house, my mother would inspect our pockets to see whether we had any of those mixed in with our haul.

Often she gave out to us, scolding, "I told ye not to be bringing in those oul' *caise púcas!*"

That was her word for them, because in Irish, *púca* means 'fungus' and sometimes it was pronounced *'coisa púca'*, which means 'fungus foot'.

CHAPTER SEVENTEEN

Going for the Cows

Tender first, the ballast train moved sleepily along the line. Arriving at each cinder box, the driver stopped and allowed my father's gang to unload the cargo that he was carrying. When the men had finished shovelling, the driver, who was obliged to sound a whistle for the safety of the milesmen below, moved off down the track. The spreading of cinders in this way helped railway stations to clear out the remnants of the coal used by the engines and on my father's section, the cinder locations were indicated by ground-level boxes made from sleepers beside the embankment.

Such trains were not allowed to run during a fog or falling snow. The weather had to be clear enough to see a signal distinctly from half a mile away. On this particular day, the sky was clear and the sweet smell of heather carried on the air from the nearby Ballinough Hills.

The men fell in – their shovels crunching loudly into the black glinting mass that the cold cinders made. As he stood by, my father removed a rolled-up copy of the Permanent Way regulations and beat it against his thigh in the rhythm of a hornpipe.

Just then, remembering something, he halted his 'regulations hornpipe' and let out a shout to the departing train driver who was our cousin Tom Gaynor.

"Hould her there a minute," he cried. Tom braked heavily in a hiss of steam, and then craned his neck over the platform. "Is anything the matter?" he shouted.

My father removed his cap and shielded his eyes with it.

"Ah, I nearly forgot," he laughed. "T'oul' Inspector and John Lynham are stopping for dinner. I better let the missus know."

While he waited, Tom decided to make a longer stop of it, so he sat on the edge of the footplate and put a kettle on the raker. When the water had boiled, he took a mouthful of tea from the mug that the fireman handed to him. Joining them, my father searched for some paper on which to scribble a note.

"Hould yer gallop there," Tom said, as he pulled out his seat box – a large oaken chest filled with spare gauge glasses, detonators, flags and spanners. He rummaged through all of these until, with a grunt of satisfaction, he retrieved some well-used rule books. Inside one of these was a loose sheaf of paper which he offered to my father with a grimy hand.

Like most people, my father used his right hand, but could write almost as well with his left. When he had finished, he wrapped the note around a piece of coal and handed it to the driver with instructions to drop it at the railway house and sound a whistle to let my mother know.

When we heard Tom Gaynor coming, we shouted that 'Nancy-loves-a-home-baked-cake' was on his way, because that was what he always said to my mother when he'd be after brown bread. With a face grimy from working on the footplate, he waved cheerily as he dropped the message.

That evening, when it was almost dark, I was told to go over to Kilmucklin for the cows. We had some fields over there that had been given to my mother grudgingly as a dowry after she got married. Since she lived in the biggest house in Kilmucklin, she was considered to have married beneath herself by marrying my father. Fortunately one of her brothers, who lived in America, came home for a holiday and found out the way that his sister was being treated. He argued that there was something wrong with the split and that she should have got her rightful share.

From that day on, we had ownership over thirteen acres – 'The Long Bog', 'Aughamore' and 'Jenny's'. The first field was so named because it brought you out to the bog. To get to the second, you had to go past the Anglican Church in Clara village and up the hill. On this particular evening however, the cows were up at Jenny's and to get to them, I had to cross the yard of an old woman called Mary Ann Delaney. 'Lord, I wonder will she come out?' I wondered. To make this happen, I decided to make a whole lot of noise with rusty buckets and discarded pots until eventually she opened the half door.

When she saw who it was, she laughed.

"Did your father tell ye to go for the cows?" she enquired.

"Yes," I smiled back shyly, half hoping that she would invite me in. I wasn't disappointed because without any ceremony, the old woman ushered me into the warm, lamp-lit kitchen. The chickens meanwhile, gazed beadily at me from their perch on the open half door.

"Chessssssssh!" Mary Ann cried and waved them out of the kitchen with her apron. Then she hobbled off to the parlour to find something for me to eat. "Sure I may as well look after you while I'm still in it," she shouted.

While she foostered away, I pulled up a bockety chair and sat down on it. After a few minutes she came out of the room with a lump of currant cake that had been left over from the Station Mass and put loads of jam on it with a dirty thumb. In my mind, I thought it was tastier than anything I got at home.

As I sat there dangling my feet on the edge of the chair, I suddenly remembered the cows. In a panic, I jumped down and said goodbye to Mary Anne. She waved to me as I ran from the half door, out into the cool evening air and down the lane towards the entrance to the field.

Coming towards nightfall, the instinct of a cow is to go into the corner of the field and lie down there until dawn. Night had almost fallen but because I couldn't see the cows from the gate, I gave up searching and came back.

Since leaving Mary Ann's house, I had been preoccupied with the thought that Joe Lynam was due to call any minute to our house from Clara with Inspector McKeown. It was a sort of crush I had, but it wasn't Joe I was after, it was his pipe. I thought he looked like a real gentleman when he smoked it. Needless to say, there were no cows to bring back as far as I was concerned because in my hurry to see Joe, I never bothered to look.

When I plodded back into the kitchen empty-handed, I almost got a boot in the tail.

"Would you ever go back and get the cows!" my father roared.

But when I turned to walk back the way I had come, it was dark and the trees on the laneway swayed in close to the roadside.

By the time I returned to the field, the two cows were waiting obediently at the gate, heads nodding in the dusk. I drove them out in front of me, locked the gate and we all set off down the empty road. The cows could do that journey with their eyes shut. They knew their own road, which was more than could be said for some of the people I met. Oul' workmen in varying degrees of drunkenness staggered past me on the road from Clara, and I was afraid of my life of them. One man lurched from one side of the road to the other yet barely noticed I was there. The cows on the other hand, had more sense. You could let them out in Kilmucklin and they'd find their way back to Ashfield. Coming along the byroad and out onto the main road, we turned past the big beech tree and came down the lane.

There was no electric light in the yard. With the aid of light from the house, I drove the two animals into the stable, closed the door behind them and went to fetch my mother from the kitchen.

"Would you ever light the lamp and hold it while I milk these cows?" she asked.

As I went to fetch the paraffin lamp, the prospects of spending the evening gazing at Joe Lynam and his pipe began to disappear under a mountain of household chores. I crossed the yard, swinging the lamp and held it steadily over my mother as she stooped down to milk the cows. Sometimes people didn't know how to milk, but she was a great hand at it. It's an awful thing to learn, because you're stuck there until it's finished, and in our house it was more or less my mother or myself who did it. I never saw the lads going out to milk, but we all took turns at holding the lantern.

The only thing I hated about milking was the wagging of the cow's tail, because it would give you a wallop if you got in the way. I smiled as I thought about the calf that once got the milk bucket stuck on its head. I remembered how it kept swinging this way and that in an attempt to free itself. After that, my thoughts took a turn. In my mind, the swish of the calf's tail melted into a lazy wisp of pipe smoke and I began to daydream about Joe Lynam again.

The rattle of milk as it hit the tin bucket brought me back to reality and when I realised how long I had been standing, I grew impatient. Although I wanted to sit inside, I knew that after my mother had finished, I would have the extra chore of cleaning the globe and filling the lamp with oil before replacing it on the hook.

"Will you hurry on?" I muttered.

As I stood out in the yard holding the light, Joe Lynam smoked away to his heart's content in the kitchen, not minding the argument that was going on over the cows. The other man at the fire, Inspector McKeown, was a middle-aged married man up from Mayo in the West of Ireland who had connections with my father through the railway.

Galvin's shop in Main Street, where the inspector had found lodgings, was generally referred to as an "atin' house' since 'bed & breakfast' was yet unheard of. McKeown was stopping above the shop and the woman of the house provided his meals. The proprietor, who did not partake of much 'atin' himself, was so thin that it once prompted a tailor to comment on the fit of his suit that, 'If it fits the tongs, it'll fit Galvin.'

When he had finished there for the evening, Inspector McKeown used to come out to our house. Despite the fact that he was a married man, he had a crush on my sister Bab and spared no expense to win her over. When his daughter, who was older than my sister, came from Mayo for a holiday, McKeown tried to keep their friendship a secret.

One afternoon, when Miss McKeown had gone shopping in Kilkenny, the Inspector brought Bab into Tullamore on the footplate of a train coming from Clara and brought her into Scally's.

"Lord isn't that a gorgeous coat?" I exclaimed when the couple finally returned. My father meanwhile, who had been mulling over his newspaper finally threw rank to the wind and stood up.

"Any coats that want to be bought here, I'll buy them," he shouted, rising up to face the Mayo man. "And you're lucky I don't give you a bledy puck across the jaw. Now g'wan out of it and take that with you!"

McKeown blanched and stammered for a few seconds, before snatching up the coat and making for the door. In a few seconds, pipe and all got the road.

A short time after that, the inspector started to do a strong line with a maid working for Galvins. My mother met him one day and said wryly, "Well you've a real beauty now."

"Ah you know, Mrs Gaynor," retorted McKeown. "Ugly people have to live too.'

CHAPTER EIGHTEEN

Digging Turf

One frosty winter night, a goods train came down the line under a starry sky, with fifty or so wagons behind it. Dan Liston, the fireman and Tony Quinlivan, the driver, stopped the engine outside the door and my father came out to meet them. Dan was the first to step down off the footplate, and he wiped his forehead roughly with a grimy hand.

"Begod its great to stand down off her for a few minutes," he puffed. "I'm priming here like there's no tomorrow."

My father smiled. The railwaymen were full of their own curious expressions that would baffle anyone else.

When Tony had checked that everything was as it should be, he lit his pipe off the smouldering end of a tarry wagon-sheet rope and followed Dan inside for a Christmas drink. Since he was a fireman, Joe volunteered to hop up onto the footplate to keep the engine running.

"Keep her at about 150lb pressure and check your quarter glass," came Tony's parting words, as Joe donned his pilot coat and scurried out the door.

Larry was in his element because he was very mechanically minded and loved engines and gadgetry. He jumped up onto the footplate and had free range over the regulator and the dials, under Joe's watchful eye of course.

Joe had started his career sweeping in the station and later became an engine cleaner. One of his duties then had been to clear and sweep down the inside of the still-hot firebox, with a wet handkerchief tied around his mouth. Tonight, he was revisiting the position of 'Steam-Riser', which was a leg up from engine cleaning and involved building enough pressure in the tender box to allow the train to leave the station.

With the train stopped, Tommie and Ned climbed onto the tender wagon in front of the engine and started throwing down coal. In those days, a ton cost £5, but despite that, it was well known for platelayer gangers to make unofficial requests to passing train drivers to drop some off as they passed a permanent way hut or house.

Meanwhile, I sat down for a while to listen to the grown-up chat around the fire.

That morning, I had a notion the men might call, particularly when my mother lifted the sloping lid and scooped enough flour for three big cakes out of the hundred-weight bin outside my room. As she worked, she taught me about what she was doing. 'The essence of the sour milk, acting with the soda causes the bread to rise,' she instructed before displaying the result of her labours on the dresser to cool – warm bread ready to be eaten by the hungry railwaymen.

As they sat around the table, eating and drinking away to their hearts' content, they talked with good humour and high spirits. Dan Liston began to relate an unusual incident in which he had been involved a couple of years before. A prize greyhound was being brought over to the West in the guard van of a train that Dan was firing. Seeing the potential of making some money, he managed to get it out of the van between stations and onto the footplate where he put it into a box and covered it with sacking. When the train reached Portarlington however, a cry went up that the dog had gone missing and the police were called. As they moved forward from the back of the train, Dan knew that the game was up and knowing he would certainly be caught, he threw the hapless animal into the fire.

We listened, enthralled by stories like that, wondering whether it really happened at all until someone said, 'Go up and get the coal.' We were filling buckets from the embankment until we were tired. It was a special type of engine coal and the minute it hit the fire, it rose a master head of steam.

"The chimley'll go a' fire!" I gasped, clasping my hand to my mouth but my father who knew better just smiled.

The goods train drivers weren't supposed to do that, and if they were caught they risked being sacked. But the inspector was just as bad because he was often in our house too, so you might ask who was going to do the sacking.

Nevertheless, we couldn't depend on going without turf altogether and nearly always had to rely on the bog for our main fuel source.

One Saturday afternoon, we were sent in our bare feet with a big can of tea and sandwiches to feed the diggers. For several evenings after the bigger farmers had finished, the lads went to the turf banks after school and now my father and our neighbours aimed to complete the work.

"Be careful childer. Stay away from them bog holes, and mind you don't end up like the drownded lad," my mother called after us.

Doury was a deep bog – 15 feet deep in places but in our haste and excitement, we paid little heed to her warnings. Although the 'drownded lad' had died when I was just five, my mother had been on her guard ever since. In general, she was suspicious of water and rivers or anything that young children might fall into.

Extending to the east, Doury bog was part of the great bog of Allen. At the edge of it were some little thatched cottages, and working the bog was how the families in them earned their living. Clara town was full of their donkeys and carts. It was no wonder that Our Blessed Lady went on an ass like that and she expecting, because donkeys are very quiet animals. Unfortunately, since they weren't as valuable as a pony or a horse, they were never fed or shod properly and I used to hate to see farmers hitting them.

On the way, we met our neighbour Joe Grennan, who, because he ate so much porridge, went by the name of 'Stirabout' Joe. Alongside him, a black, white-spotted donkey pulled a cart stacked high with turf.

Although it was too early for the scent of yellow heather, tufts of early summer bog cotton waved gently in the breeze. On our way to meet the men, we crossed the many small midge-filled streams that ran everywhere and searched for frogs in bog holes, but that was rather dangerous. As we walked, the small prints of our feet left marks in the soft turf.

"They're my feet, Cat," Larry shouted, as we scrambled through a clump of black bog rushes.

"They are not," I insisted. "They're mine."

I pointed to the marks behind me, but in reality it was nearly impossible to tell since we were all in the bare ones.

The cry of the corncrake was the grandest sound and we had an old cant that we chanted when we heard it – *the corncrake put out her bake and bid us all good morrow*. It couldn't sing and was more likely to be heard in a bog land. It would be impossible for me to attempt to tell you how it sounded, but it had a harsh *crawk* like a crow.

When we reached the spot that was being worked, my father and brothers were digging hard with *sléans*. The sléan was the quarest thing I ever saw. It was a handled implement with a square-shaped metal piece on the end for getting a good cut into the soggy turf.

The men kept digging until they had reached what was known locally as 'stone' turf. It was so named because of its hard, black substance and it lay underneath the yellow-coloured layers near the surface. They knew that they had reached this when peaty water began to come in under the bank.

When they had finished cutting, the men opened the sandwiches that my mother had made and boiled up the tea on a little fire.

"Begod, but that woman of yours can make a quare sandwich altogether," said Tom Robbins as he munched on the best of our ham.

Satisfied that the tea had stewed long enough, he poured out a cup for himself.

"Sure we were falling out of our stan'in', until the childer arrived," he said, casting a friendly glance in our direction.

"Now Tom, the next thing we may do is to put an oul' match on top of that tae," my father said crisply, standing and looking about.

"I'm there a'fore ye," our neighbour replied slowly, dropping a long splinter onto the bubbling brew. "That it may keep the smoky taste off of it."

After lunch, my father showed my brothers how to make the turf into stooks so that the air could reach it and allow it to dry.

"Begod," he said finally, having waited for them to get into a rhythm with their work. "Ye're stacking away there be the new time. It won't be long now at all."

Knowing that they would need to return after a few weeks to stack the smaller sods, he hoped that the rain would keep off and allow it to dry out.

When evening came, we filed back across the railway line – our tired, but happy feet leaving wet prints on the wooden sleepers. A loud creaking sound came from the track as the metal cooled, letting us know that it was time to come home. It also reminded my father that his gang would be hard at it the next day, knocking wooden keys back into place all along the line.

Meanwhile, my mother was waiting with plenty of brown bread and mugs of tea for the workers who came behind us.

In the days after the cutting, someone would have to go over to the bog with a shovel or a four-pronged pitchfork to turn the top part of the turf that had already dried. After about three weeks, when it had dried sufficiently, my father would borrow a donkey and car to bring it home for clamping in the yard. The clamp of turf, stacked similarly to a tram of hay, ensured that we had enough fuel to last throughout the winter.

CHAPTER NINETEEN

Christmas Time

In order to pay the gangs of milesmen between Kingsbridge and Athlone, Number 24, an old grey-coloured train called the *Sprite*, used to come down the line. It was a very fast engine and it carried the weekly wages in a guarded, specially furnished car. Nicknamed the 'Pay Train' by local railwaymen, it was so fast on account of the engine being rebuilt with a new kind of heater.

Payday was on Friday and when the *Sprite* reached Clara, there was a certain formality to be observed. My father – the platelayer ganger, was the first of the fourteen men to collect his money from the company clerk. He climbed into the car where a little table had been rigged up, and watched as the clerk dutifully counted out the notes and coins until it amounted to eighteen shillings. Once he had finished, the rest of the men could get their own wages.

One Friday, when the *Sprite* had met the men beyond Tullamore, it began to get up enough steam to reach the gang on the next stretch of track near Clara. Meanwhile, at home in Ashfield, my mother had been fattening fowl all year to sell for the feast of Christmas. That meant that she would have extra grocery money, especially with Ciss expected up from Dublin.

I don't remember her going to sell the birds at the fair. Instead, a buyer would come out to settle with her for the turkeys and if she was lucky she could fetch well over a shilling per pound each for them. Those would sell then for two shillings and four pence per pound in the town. One or two were kept for the Christmas table, and Bab was great at looking after them during the year.

Occasionally, a disease known as the 'pick' would do the rounds and our fowl sometimes caught it. Choked by a worm stuck in its throat, the afflicted bird would walk around the yard making coughing sounds, but Bab always knew what to do to save its life. First she would restrain the chicken by holding it between her knees. Then, using an old tail feather, she would wind the worm out of its throat. After that, the bird would cluck happily around the yard.

But there were other times when my mother, busy with her own preparations, would ask, 'Will you go out and pull the head of that chicken?' Bab was sent because she also had the most skill at killing and plucking.

On the day that the *Sprite* was due, we had about 15 turkeys ready for selling but there was no one minding them. The big yard gate had been left open and as the morning drew on, they moved into the laneway and onto the line. Soon the whole gang of them was pecking away between the sleepers, not paying heed to anyone.

After coming down the incline, there were only about 700 yards of track along which the driver could see the birds, but he closed the distance too quickly to do anything about it. In a split second, the *Sprite* came up on top of them, while we looked on in horror. With a grinding noise, the pummel of the engine's slide valves slowed to a stop and a few seconds later, the feather-choked wheels came to a standstill.

When he realised what had happened, the driver of the *Sprite* jumped off the footplate and ran into our kitchen. Hesitantly, he approached my mother with his cap in his hands.

"Er…hello missus," he stumbled. "I'm terrible sorry for what happened to yer birds."

My mother looked at him helplessly.

"Musha, stop," she replied, almost in a whisper.

For a long time after the *Sprite* had pulled away, she sat in the kitchen crying bitterly.

"Go up and bring down them fowl," she sobbed.

Feeling sorry for her predicament, we gathered as many bodies as we could in our small arms and walked down the line with them. In the end, she decided to give what was left of the turkeys to the neighbours, since they were supposed to be for Christmas but had gone up in smoke.

Besides turkeys, we kept other animals that had to be fattened for the Christmas season. Once, a neighbouring farmer had a sow pig that had just given birth, but there was one piglet too many and being the runt of the litter, it couldn't find a place on its mother's teat to suck. The farmer offered the animal to my father and we kept it in an aerated box beside the fire. It soon began to thrive on milk from a bottle until one day it started to lift the lid of the box with its snout. When that happened, my mother decided that it was strong enough to go into one of the outhouses on its own.

After that, I was told that I owned the pig and could keep it as a pet. Once it had been nursed back to health, my job was to fatten it up with cabbages, potatoes and oats, and when it was sold I would get all the money. Then, one night in October, my parents had a private discussion and although I strained to listen through the wall, I could hear nothing.

The following afternoon, Patrick Fox – a farmer from Tara and a great friend of ours – arrived out to the house and after having a cup of tea in the kitchen, he set to work. I looked out from my bedroom window near the little basin, full of curiosity about what was about to happen. My mother, on the other hand, was running up the chimney or anywhere she could go.

The fasting pig was driven, squealing, up from the yard to where the turf clamp was. Next, I saw Patrick ready with a big mallet to stun it. He gave it a whallop on the forehead and it went down heavily on its side. Then, taking a long knife in his hand, he stuck it in the throat and stripped it down, catching the blood in a basin. The pig was as dead as a doornail then.

Now you couldn't kill a pig and eat it straight away. Patrick's training as a butcher put a lot of business his way in the months before Christmas, and his skill in killing and cutting the meat was highly sought after. With his help, the hams were salt-cured outside in a big-handled basin and then hung up. The ribs, ears and other leftovers were brought around in a big bucket to neighbours and we used the blood for making oaten meal black pudding.

In mid-December, we started to decorate the house to have it nice for the twenty-fifth. Skipping across the track, we went to collect a big bundle of green holly and ivy from Doury. As we walked, I chanted:

Ivy brought to the wood,
And ivy brought back home by the lug.

Returning to the house, we took bits off the bundle and busied ourselves putting it behind pictures and rising dust. It would only stay there for a short time because Christmas was over very quickly in our house. While it lasted however, the holiday was a time for food and for diversion of every description. A candle in the window meant that our Lord was coming and that a light was coming into the world even in the short days of winter. It was also a sign of welcome to travellers and ramblers – the very ones who needed no invitation at any other time during the year. We used to love it because you'd see that glow coming from the little window as you turned off the main road and came down the laneway. If it was 'sneacthin' out, the little light shone up the lane like something straight out of a Christmas card.

One December morning, I had a big fire lighting and was busying myself with doing up the house. Before going to bed the night before, my mother had damped the fire down, burying a couple of live embers in the middle. When I got up, I removed the 'griosach', which were the dead ashes of the hearth. Then I took out the live embers and used the bellows Larry had made to fan them into a new fire.

The dresser made by my grandfather, Joe Gaynor, was in the middle of the kitchen and I was very busy cleaning it out, dusting in behind where all the cups and delph sat. When I had finished, I carefully lifted down the big oval goose dish from where it had lain all year and used some water from the barrel outside to wash it down. With the dust gone, the blue willow-pattern shone through like new.

An hour or so passed and my mother got up to dress herself at the fire. Going to bed, she used to let her hair down, and in the morning time it would be down to her shoulders and very curly. Then she'd comb it, put it into a bun at the back and fasten it with a large pin.

As I worked, I suddenly got a strong smell of singeing, so I looked around and was shocked to see that my mother's hair had caught fire without her realising. In my hurry to put it out, I never considered my own safety. I patted her head quickly with my hands until the room filled with smoke and then cried out with the pain. Coughing from the fumes, I flung the kitchen door open and plunged my hands into the cool water of the barrel.

My mother meanwhile, waved the smoke away with a cloth, marvelling at how she hadn't felt a thing because she had her hair down. When she realised that I was burnt however, she took fright and called for my father who took me straight down to Pettitt's.

"Oh Lord!" the chemist exclaimed when he saw me coming. "What happened to your hands?" I told him the story and I had my hands in bandages for weeks afterwards.

As young children, we never had Santa Claus or anything like that. That was just for the town children. Instead, my father used to bring us down to the railway hut at Christmas and Easter. With a wink, he would say, 'Come on, I'll bring ye down to the shop.' After rummaging for the key in the kitchen drawer, he would beckon to us to follow him down the line.

There were huts along every three miles of track and ours, like many others, was made from sleepers set standing upright. The floor was made from the same material. Inside, the hut smelled of creosote and it contained all sorts of iron wrenches, some of which had been borrowed from what was once the MG&WR line going to Mullingar. It also held shovels, crowbars, jacks, keying hammers, spanners and ballast forks. There were also scythes for keeping hedges and grass trimmed back from the track and a whetstone for sharpening them.

When we went in, my father had put sweets and cakes on some of the shelves, and occasionally he would leave some little toys that he had bought from Kenny's shop in Bridge Street. Kenny was a great salesman, who found it easy to dupe my father once he had a few drinks on him! We thought the visit to the hut was great, which of course it was because we used our imagination.

On Christmas Eve, which was my father's birthday, some men from Dinny Nicholson's gang arrived to whitewash the house. During the year, Larry had gone with his pal Johnnie Sheridan to help Dinny and his gang paint railway bridges on the section. The men had made ready to lower a gantry over the side of the bridge and the boys' job was to stand down on the roadway with a red flag to warn any oncoming traffic that the headroom had been lowered.

The railway house presented no difficulty to these seasoned painters. Number 225 was the last to receive the 'cat's lick' and the men were in high spirits. The G.S.R. paid for the operation and it was normally completed twice a year. Marshalling the lads in the yard, the ganger bid the men prepare some buckets. Water was added to the chalky lime until, when tested with a stick, it had a consistency of paint.

Then, each armed with a horse-hair brush, the milesmen carried the heavy, sloshing buckets around to the front of the house. Starting there, they whitewashed the walls until they gleamed like new. Nobody thought to wish my father a happy birthday – least of all my mother, because birthdays were rarely celebrated in those days.

Instead, she knelt by the bed and said a Novena to pray for good weather so that she could get to second Mass on Christmas morning. The previous year, the weather had been so bad that she had to say her prayers in the house instead. On Christmas Eve, we were supposed to fast from midnight until midday on Sunday, but half the time we only let on to do it.

"It's a shame for ye," my mother lamented, before going to bed that night starving with the hunger.

On Christmas morning, her prayers were answered. With no ice on the ground, the trap was prepared and we set out through the dark for eight o'clock Mass. Coaxing the pony up the hill at Berrigan's corner, my father picked his way warily, straining his eyes past the glow of the carbide lamps in an effort to keep the wheels from tumbling into the dike. In his care to watch the road, he almost missed my Aunt Delia, who was making her way through the dim morning light from the big house in Kilmucklin. When he pulled the pony up, she lifted her long black skirt and climbed the metal step. With a switch of the reins, we set off again.

During her youth, Delia had lived in Dublin, where she worked for the drapery section of Pym's. Eventually, she came home to marry Ned Burke, but their relationship quickly soured and she called him 'Oul' Hooves' on account of his hobble. Many's the evening that she arrived in tears at our door in the middle of a card game or music session, and my mother was obliged to put her up for the night.

As a result, Delia had an insight into the goings on at our house and as she settled into the trap, she gave my mother a rub.

"Ah," she sneered above the clatter of the wheels, "you're alright now; you're in with all the Clashawauns."

Young as I was, I knew that her remark was directed at Bill Fleming and the 'Scutter' Kelly – two musicians who were due to arrive at our house that evening.

Fleming and Kelly were from a district in the town where the jute factory workers lived, and although they had plenty of money and were beautifully dressed, they had no land. According to the local farmers, that meant they were poverty stricken and Delia held the same view.

"You'll soon have the Slammons as well," she said, drawing herself up haughtily. Then, reading from my mother's expression that her sister knew the rumours about how the Slammon women plied themselves amongst the overnighting train drivers, she turned her face away and said no more. Meanwhile, my mother seethed with anger and was on the verge of putting Delia out of the car. No one was ever good enough for the Burkes and there were a lot like her who looked down on the people of Clashawaun – a class of people who were full of music.

Soon, the trap was rattling past the dark wooden-shuttered shops of Main Street. Before reaching the spire-less church, my father twitched the reins and the pony turned left into White's yard. With a few minutes to spare, he and my mother shook hands with our neighbours at the door of the church and thanked God that they were in it for another year. Then my father blessed himself at the font and walked ahead of us to usher my mother and Aunt Delia into a pew.

As we waited for the service to begin, my mother – still annoyed with her sister – opened her prayer book and placed it on the pew beside her. The purpose of the book was to help her to follow the priest in English. It told her for instance that *'Misereatur tui omnipotens Deus'* meant *'May Almighty God have mercy on you,'* prompting her to utter a pious 'Amen' in the right place.

I broke into a mischievous smile and wondered what would happen if she couldn't follow the priest, so when she wasn't looking I turned the page. When Mass began, she was sure to lose her place. Spotting me out of the corner of her eye, she turned sharply.

"What did you do that for?" she snapped.

But there was no time for an argument and we had to stand with the rest of the congregation while the priest and two servers came out of the sacristy. Standing with his back to the people, he genuflected on the first step while the servers knelt below. Fluidly, he made the Sign of the Cross and uttered the words: *'In nomine Patris, et Filii, et Spiritus Sancti.'*

The nuns had come to the same Mass and a place was set aside for them in the chapel. Arriving by a separate entrance, they were ushered into red velvet-curtained nooks where they sat away from the congregation. When I looked carefully, I could see their veils peeping out. These were the same nuns who taught me at school, and those who had attended first Mass had received communion from the side altar.

During the service, collection baskets were sent around and Aunt Delia gave with great ceremony. Christmas was perhaps the only time of the year that such a collection was made inside Clara church, and she wasn't going to lose the chance to be seen giving her contribution to the Priests' Money. On the Sunday after Christmas, Father Bracken would read the names aloud, starting with the highest donation and finishing with the smallest – 'Doctor O'Hara, £2; Sam Clyne, £1 and ten pence.' Somewhere down the list, he would reach my father and his neighbours who always gave half a crown each.

****

That afternoon, my father carved the goose while my mother bustled and fussed until we all had hot, steaming plates in front of us. Once she was sure that we were all looked after, she sat down herself. But when we were finished, we began to ask for more. 'That's flying in God's face,' she reproached mildly. 'Thank God for what you have, and thank him you're able to move.' My mother had so many of us that there was no such thing as favourites, so we accepted the lesson grudgingly.

When dinner was over, my father got out what he called 'The Jug', a big three-quart barrel of 'Double X' with a grey strip at one end and green at the other and stamped with White's' label. It had been delivered a week or so earlier by shop boy Peter Rattigan, along with the rest of our Christmas order.

"Well Missus, will you take a drop in a mug?" he asked coaxingly.

"Arra sure I might as well,' my mother answered. "But only seeing as it's Christmas."

My father duly obliged, but when he noticed how quickly the porter went flat after opening, he took the poker from the hearth and plunged it inside the jar. Before long, it frothed up again and he re-corked the mulled contents. 'I'll hould onto the rest of that until them all comes down afterwards,' he said.

That night, there were so many people in our house that it was uncertain as to who was inviting whom. Some came on bicycles and others by foot. Bill Fleming himself walked out along the railway from Clashawaun with his pal Scutter Kelly, the latter having received his nickname on account of the fact that he was so mean looking. Soon the bush-choked lane filled with the sound of wheels and if there weren't enough people besides the crowd of ramblers, they were obliged to share the hearth with my mother and father, a gang of children and a dog.

Joining the rest of the musicians on the settle bed, Bill took out his accordion, which we looked forward to because it was like a band in itself. My father played the melodeon for amusement and his pal Jack Delaney, a farmer's son, was a great flute player.

My father was a real master and in his younger days had been greatly sought after at house dances for his musical skill. As he played, people placed drink in front of him, but he got lost in the music and never touched a drop. Soon the whole table was covered in glasses. When that happened, Mike Doorley lifted a full glass and replaced it with a half-empty one of his own. My father, engrossed in his playing, never noticed.

The melodeon is a very difficult instrument to master, because you have to squeeze both sides and get different notes on the out breath than you do on the in. The piano accordion, on the other hand is something that only requires the musician to squeeze with one hand while the other selects the notes.

Together with the other musicians, he played the reels 'Drowsy Maggie' and 'Roaring Mary' and then two of Jack's favourites – a double jig called 'Tumble the Tinker' and a jig called 'The Cat that Ate the Candle'. When Larry joined them on the accordion, a workman for Wogan's got out in the middle of the floor and jumped about excitedly shouting, 'Holy Jerusalem, Jumping Johnny!'

But then panic ensued. Georgie Bannon had been spotted coming down the lane and my father, recalling previous visits, was sure the thatcher was going to take up his melodeon and pull the guts out of it.

"Look what's at the gate!" he shouted, thrusting the two-stoppered instrument into my small hands. I had to run to find a hiding place before it was too late.

Afterwards, my parents decided that the table and dresser should be pulled out of the way to make room for dancing. They had been great dancers from their youth, and soon we had a full set with eight people on the floor. Some favourites were the 'Walls of Limerick' and the 'Siege of Ennis' and although we had a concrete floor, so much dust was raised by the pounding feet that my mother had to open the door at intervals to let it out.

There was tea in the parlour room then, followed by some slow airs and a chance for somebody to sing. A favourite of my father's was a comic song called 'Sweet Killarney', and it concerned the wistful longings of a man long past his infanthood. Grasping his braces with both hands, he began:

> *I was born in sweet Killarney,*
> *One day when I was young,*
> *And that is just the reason,*
> *Why the Blarney is on my tongue.*

> *Now the night was dark and stormy,*
> *And the rain came pouring down,*
> *And the old nurse Judy Kearney,*
> *Lived a long way out of town.*

> *Sure my father got the donkey out,*
> *And off went in a crack,*
> *Judy sat beside him,*
> *And he very soon came back.*

> *I was a pretty baby,*
> *All the neighbours would allow,*
> *They brought the girls to kiss me,*

But I wish they'd do it now!

Later on, all the lads lined up along the sideboard in the porch and played away. In those days there was a single engine that we used to call 'The Paper Train' because it carried all the daily newspapers to the towns along the line. That was due in at about two or three o'clock in the morning. and sometimes Tommie would have to be on hand to meet it when it arrived at Clara. Leaving Tullamore, it used to go like a bullet to Clara because it wasn't shunting any wagons.

Although our house was only about twelve feet from the railway embankment, we never heard the trains at night because we were reared up to it, but the visitors from town were a different matter. When the paper train eventually passed, the *chtch-e chtch-e* of the wheels rattled the cups on the dresser, making the whole house shake. The musicians grabbed their hats and jumped for cover because they thought it was coming through the kitchen.

Laughing, Tommie took out his Jew's harp and Larry took up a fiddle that had been discarded during the panic. He could play it by ear and ruined me because I had the right position and was learning it professionally at Mrs Molloy's school. In fact, some of the old ramblers who came in had a rhyme about the fiddle that stuck in our heads and we often recited it as children:

This is the way my father showed me how to play the fiddle'o,
Here and there and everywhere but especially in the middle'o!

There is a way of holding the instrument so that you aren't gripping the bow, but are holding it down to give yourself the whole length of the string. But Larry took it up any way to make music.

When I eventually got a chance to play, Larry cried, "That one'll need the whole kitchen cleared."

He meant that I would need enough room to draw the bow, but

my father put his hand out and said, "Leave her now. Let her play." With that, I started with 'The Harvest Home', followed by 'Mrs McLeod's Reel'.

"Begod, Mrs McLeod's hornpipe is a grand tune," enthused Joe Finn.

The mistake called to mind an earlier visit during which he played a reel on the fiddle but after a few minutes, made no sign of turning it. He kept playing the same notes over and over again, so my father turned to him when he was finished and said wryly, "That's a grand tune you just played. That's the very same now as the Banagher railway."

Joe thought that he was being paid a compliment but Mr Finn knew what my father was getting at. The Banagher railway had a reputation for being one of the straightest pieces of track in Ireland and there were no turns in it.

But I'm forgetting the gramophone, and no talk of Christmas would be complete without mentioning it. Ours was *His Master's Voice*, which my father put into the parlour room for his own entertainment. It had a big horn on it and a handle that you had to wind to keep the music going. Fully wound, a metal switch kept the music from starting until you were ready. Once it was turned on however, the crackling echo of Jimmy O'Dea's voice ascended from the horn, filling the little room:

> '*Does yer brother ate onions?*'
> '*I haven't got a brother.*'
> (Pause)
> '*Well if you had a brother, would he ate them?*'

When it was holiday time, I loved to light a fire in the parlour and bring in bread and butter as though I was a visitor. In there, we had all the records, such as 'Happy Days Are Here Again' and later on, some of Bing Crosby's songs. A favourite of mine was 'Home on the Range'.

The wireless came in a few years after that. A railwayman called Tommy Lenny, who looked after the telegraph poles between stations, passed our house one wet morning. Over a cup of tea, he explained to my father and Larry the makings of a crystal set.

After breakfast, they sat down to copy exactly what Tommy had shown them. First, my father ran an aerial out from the house and up into one of Mike Doorley's trees, taking care to insulate the wire at certain points. Next, he went into Clara to buy a wet and dry battery and a crystal which sat on a tripod. One of the main parts was called a 'LEM' box – a contraption that had a piece of tin at each end, wrapped in a coil of two-inch thick wire. A wire went to the LEM box and one to the headset, completing the radio.

In those early days, having paid the ten-bob licence fee, we just picked up Athlone. It wasn't long however before we were listening to matches broadcast from Croke Park.

One day, my father tapped the side of the radio and found that the reception was very weak.

"God dammit to hell," he muttered to himself, carefully removing the wet battery from its housing with a delicate hand. "Cat, would ye ever cycle in as far as town with that?"

Landed rightly with the job, I set off for Stephen Fitz's shop in River Street. There, I handed in the old battery, balanced the new one in my carrier and began the slow journey back to Ashfield, carefully navigating between the potholes. But that idea went to hell altogether when the front wheel suddenly slipped from under me, jostled the carrier basket and broke the contents. As the acid began to leak out, it dripped onto the side of my beautiful long coat and burned it. It was destroyed and I roared and bawled over it.

****

Besides music and dancing, people used to gather at Christmas to play cards where the usual stakes were raised, and a turkey or chicken was played for. Local policeman Tom Hunt was a regular at our table. One day, beginning to despair of ever issuing a prosecution, he went to a farmer's field and quietly drove out all the cattle. After waiting to make sure that the animals were far enough along the road and getting into every place they shouldn't be, the policeman knocked on the half door.

"Are those your cattle?" he asked, knowing well he had let them out himself.

"I suppose they are," answered the flustered farmer, who stood scratching his head.

Once Tom had a summons for the court, he could go back to playing Twenty-Five. It could be played by up to six people but occasionally it was played by eight people or four partners. In starting a game, the Joker was always taken out of the deck, because the old people believed that a Joker was the sign of the devil. That was just an oul' piserog, but in any case he wasn't worth anything. The game of cards was lovely, but there were often shocking rows over tricks and reneging.

The lesser in black and the more in red – that was the lesson of cards. Someone might play a heart but the man sitting next to him, knowing that his heart led, would hold onto it until the end of the game. In the meantime, he would put any card out and shuffle his heart up. In an effort to renege, he would do his level best to stop the rest of the table from seeing his hand. However, if he wasn't careful enough, someone would spot the hidden heart and a serious row would start.

Sometimes people wouldn't speak for weeks over the difference of a few cards. One evening at our house, the big table was pulled out and a farmer's son from the locality sat down with Larry to play Twenty-Five. From his place in the corner, Tommie watched his brother closely because our neighbour could buy and sell the likes of poor Lar, even though he was working and had plenty of money. The rubber was worth a pound a man, which in those days was an awful lot.

They played on until eventually the farmer hit the table with his cards and gathered up his winnings. Tommie was disgusted, because he was very solid in character and didn't like to see Larry being outdone. When he had gone, the tea was made and the two lads debated on the card game.

"You made a mistake there with that,"'Tommie muttered. "You threw out a pound, but you might as well have thrown it into the fire."

He was disgusted because there had been so much money involved. With that, Larry, who was always very hotheaded and lavish with money, put his hand into his pocket and pulled out the last pound he had.

"Will you shut up," he shouted. "That's what I think about it!" and he pegged it into the hearth.

I'd an awful job trying to get it out. Oh Jaysus, I saw it going in and I nearly burnt myself trying to get it with the long tongs. I never got pocket money so a pound was a great prize.

Now, I laughed to myself, *ye fought about it. Well I have it now!*

CHAPTER TWENTY

Hunting the Wren

When I was growing up, it was the tradition to go hunting the wren after Christmas. My mother and father would say 'Oh God, the Wran Boys will be around today!' and that would be their enjoyment. Wearing visards with big noses and straw hats, they would start after first Mass on Stephen's Day and wouldn't finish their rounds until late in the evening. Although they were all neighbours, we never recognised the Wren Men when they came into the house. After they had danced a half set on the country floor, one of the group would chant a rhyme that was well known to both young and old:

> *The Wran, the Wran, the king of all birds,*
> *St Stephen's Day he was caught in the furze,*
> *Although he was little his family was great,*
> *Get up young lady and give us a trate.*
> *Up with the kettle and down with the pan,*
> *A penny or tuppence to bury the Wran.*

As the rhyme was being chanted, one of their number would go about the kitchen with a hat, which he held out for money. If there was a hooley in one of the houses, they used to leave that for the last and stay there for the night. At that house, the masks would be removed and you'd know them then as neighbours.

One Stephen's Day, Lar and I got permission to dress up as

Wran Boys on the condition that we only did a few houses and didn't go into town. Delighted with ourselves, we borrowed baggy old trousers and disguised ourselves as best we could. Like Larry, I wore an old hat belonging to my father and a mask made out of paper with a big ugly face and red crepe tongue. Our neighbours wouldn't know who it was no more nor cock robin. When we were ready, Larry took down the accordion and we set off up the lane. Going from house to house, we got lovely cake and lemonade, but we never made ourselves known.

Later that evening, we arrived at a thatched house with a big stone floor. Inside, an old couple and their neighbours had gathered at the fire to talk and smoke clay pipes. Without announcing ourselves, we pushed the half door open and Lar started to play a hornpipe. I got out on the floor in my bare feet and you never saw such dancing. With great excitement, the old man rose off his seat.

"Come quick Biddy, till you see this," he cried.

A woman emerged from a bedroom beside the fire and pressed her hands to her face.

"Oh Jaysus Christ," she exclaimed. "Isn't she something?"

Soon the kitchen came alive as the men began to beat blackthorn sticks against the ground to keep time with the music.

As small as I was, I was thrilled to be out on the floor dancing with this crowd cheering us on. After a while however, one of the neighbours took a guess as to who we were. Our bare feet were what gave it away.

"I'm telling you who it is," he whispered to the old woman and she looked at my ankles and nodded her head in agreement. Suddenly, the man made a drive at me in an attempt to pull my mask off, but I was quicker than he was. As nimble as a rabbit, I ducked underneath his legs and ran off as if the devil himself were behind me.

CHAPTER TWENTY-ONE

The Dublin Jackeen

Every year on the ninth of June, crowds flocked to the Pattern of Durrow. It was a big event for the little village because it was there that St Columcille had supposedly put his cross in the ground. Water sprung from the spot the cross struck and it became a place of pilgrimage thereafter. The saint carried it from I don't know where but the sweat must have been rolling off him because we had a job cycling to it every year.

On the morning of the pattern, I was feeding fowl in the little yard at the back of the house when my mother shouted to me from the open door. "Get me a sup of Colmcille's holy water at the well and I'll give you the bottle."

A workman had been down to the railway house a few days before, and when my mother enquired after his sick mother, he replied that she was very 'donny'. Since the woman had weakened so much, she thought immediately of the holy water as a cure.

I was expecting my boyfriend Tommy Feehan any minute, but as I continued feeding the chickens, I was suddenly aware of someone else watching me. I looked up to catch the gaze of a well-dressed young man leaning on the handlebars of a racer. Besides his new sports coat, he was wearing plus fours – an awful, but expensive type of trousers where the legs came down to a band at the knee. We smiled at each other.

The young man was none other than Martin Dalton, a Dublin lad I had my eye on from the previous summer and, needless to say, I was delighted.

"How are you Cat?" he shouted over from the lane.

"I'm grand," I said. "Are you only coming now?"

"Ah no," Martin replied. "I cycled down yesterday evening."

It had been a warm summer night when he finally reached his Aunt Mary Anne Delaney's house, but despite being tired from the journey, he couldn't wait to see me. I chatted away with him and let on that I was very sophisticated.

Suddenly my father let a roar. "Come *down* and give this oul' pig something to eat!" he bellowed.

Our sow was nearly coming out under the door with the hunger, but since I wanted to let on that I was a girl who never fed pigs or fowl, I just blushed ashamedly at Martin.

When I returned indoors, my father glared at me over the newspaper.

"Do you mind telling me what that feckin' egit wanted?" he asked. "He's there one minute and gone the next." But being the quare hawk that I was, I didn't let on I knew anything.

Then Tommy arrived so we all set off, crunching our wheels over the fallen seeds of the old beech tree. Martin cycled with one arm on the racer's handlebars and the other around me, while Tommy brought up the rear with an old High Nellie that Ned had resurrected from the sheds.

All the way to Durrow, the ditches were a white carpet of cow parsley and an occasional rabbit scurried across our hilly path, gunning for the hedge on the far side. We pedalled on for a while until, passing through a crossroads, the land fell away below us for miles and we could see wisps of smoke rising from tiny houses. To our right, the heather-covered hills of the esker rose into the hazy summer sky.

With a cheerful wave, other young people passed on bicycles and we met traps and carts of all descriptions. Tommy however did not share their sentiment. He could see what was going on between me and Martin and was becoming more disgusted as the miles passed.

Cycling up alongside me Ned said, "Tommy is raging. He says he'll kill that fella." But I ignored the remark.

"Tell *Tommy* I want holy water," I said dismissively, throwing my eyes skyward.

Ned fell behind to relay my answer and then returned with a reply. "He says he'll get it for you, but he'll feck that fella into the well with you."

As we approached Durrow, the ridge of the esker gave way to pockets of woodland and we cycled through the iron entrance gates and filed down a long avenue. As the trees closed in on both sides, cool air bellowed around us until suddenly the woods thinned out and the old churchyard lay to our right.

A lot of the older people were already there when we arrived, kneeling down amongst the stones or buying from the small group of tinkers who stood nearby with sugarstick sweets and all sorts of accoutrements. At the lower end of the old graveyard was a high cross decorated with worn carvings of Daniel and the Lion and other stories we recognised from our school days. People came from miles around to attempt to span the cross, but I barely managed to get my arms around it.

Standing nearby was a lad from East Wall in Durrow who I used to go with called Hughie Murray. Out of earshot of the others, I laughingly told him about the difficult bicycle journey that we had had that morning, and that Martin Dalton ought to be in the well by now. When he heard what Tommy had said, Hughie shook his head solemnly.

"Well, there was *gravel* in that remark," he muttered.

"Oh duck you, bugger duck," I said between my teeth, as Tommy suddenly approached. Snatching the empty bottle from my hand in front of Hughie, he cast the two of us a foul look and stormed off towards the holy well.

There, on a slab covered by stones was an inscription:

St Colmcille used this well when he preached the Gospel and built an Abbey nearby: A.D. 550

As we sat down to rest after our cycle, I lay back against one of the many yew trees planted in rows all over the cemetery. Shading my eyes with my hands, I watched the people as they knelt and prayed on their bare knees.

Farmers believed that the well could cure anything, so they'd travel from miles around to get a drop of St Colmcille's water from it. For them, it was a very useful thing to have about the house. In an emergency, they would lift down the bottle from some hidden place and shake it over a sick cow whereas in reality, it was the vet they needed.

As a child, I remember a neighbour who was very sick so they used to bring him in to a quack doctor, because they believed in his ability to cure a person. They were harmless that way. The 'doctor' was an oul' lad who set up a clinic in his yard where there was a well and was supposed to be able to cure someone if they went there three times.

The patient had what people called 'Sleepy Sickness', which was very prevalent at that time. It caused extreme tiredness and the poor man, who hadn't the strength to work his land, became bedridden in the house. Three times he was carried into the doctor's yard and three times the crowd followed him. Well, they didn't leave a sup of water in the well. The old people had other such *piseróg s* (superstitions), but no matter what they were told to the contrary, they still believed in it.

There was certainly no telling my mother any different, and

when Tommy returned from the well, I carefully re-corked the bottle. As we returned from Durrow that evening, we met a group of children in the lane near the railway house. Smiling, I doled out the last of our sugarstick sweets and recalled how people returning on bikes had done the same for me when I was a child. Eventually, tired but happy, we reached the railway house. Resting our bikes on the railings, we opened the gate and walked up the path. My mother had already gone to bed, so I left the little bottle of holy water on the table for her when she woke up the next morning.

CHAPTER TWENTY-TWO

Father Troy

'Oh she'll be killed!' Ned Robbins gasped, blessing himself. Tommy Feehan had arrived to take me on a date, but hadn't realised how interested I would be in his motorbike. Impatient to drive it, I had taken off too fast and headed straight for a big, bush-clogged drain at the gate.

Once the dust had settled, Tommy showed me how to kickstart the engine. By working the clutch with my left hand and gears with my foot, I had a couple of practice lessons up and down the lane. After a while, I felt confident enough and I took off with a roar towards the Tullamore Road – the bike sounding louder than it should have on account of the fact that I didn't have the silencers on. I drove up past Berrigan's and along the dusty road in front of Aunt Delia's house, waving cheekily at the cold windows. Finally, I came back down the hill past Johnstons'. As I passed their orchard, I imagined that the old couple's Protestant manners and perhaps their apples might be severely rattled by the sight of me flying past on a motorbike.

By the time I returned down the lane, the shadows were beginning to lengthen and the Red Indian badge, which had gleamed at the start of my jaunt, was covered in dust. Ned and Ellen Robbins stood anxiously with my mother – their poor hearts almost about to give way for worry.

After parking Tommy's bike, we walked out into the countryside and found a hollow where we could chat away until darkness fell. We were lying there when suddenly we saw the big cartwheel arc of a light bobbing up and down in the distance and we decided to hide. I knew it must be Larry on his way home because he had a dynamo lamp that you could see for miles on a dark country road.

When I came home, my mother and father were sitting around by the fire with a few neighbours and Larry was playing the accordion. When I lifted the latch, he changed suddenly from playing a hornpipe and struck up an air that my boyfriend was well known for singing ('The Irish Peasant Girl' by Charles J. Kickham):

> *She lived beside the Anner at the foot of Slievenaman,*
> *A gentle peasant girl with mild eyes like the dawn.*
> *Her lips were dewy rosebuds, her teeth of pearls rare,*
> *And a snowdrift 'neath a beechen bough, her neck and nut-brown hair.*

For a minute, the crowd at the fire was surprised at the sudden change in the music, but they quickly took to the new tune and enjoyed it. In one stroke Larry let me know that he had caught me out since only I knew that the air was meant for us.

Mostly however, Larry got it the same as I did because we were very close in age growing up. One night, my father, hearing him come in, took his pocket watch off the headboard. When he saw that it was three o'clock, he roared: "You've no respect for her or yourself, whoever she is!"

Then, dressed in his long johns he came out into the kitchen to confront his son.

"Is that all the thanks I get for rearing you?" he shouted.

"Who asked you to?" Larry said.

All the arguing made Tommie stir from his sleep. Opening one eye, he glanced sleepily at the two men.

"Passion Father," he said sternly, before turning over again.

Afterwards, Lar came in and stood at the foot of my bed.

"Wouldn't that sicken you?" he muttered. "I wouldn't mind, only I was just out playing cards with Stephen Fitz."

Meanwhile, my father could still be heard grumbling to my mother in the room next door. Not wanting to get myself into trouble, I sat up in bed and hissed: "Would you go out or you'll end up getting me into trouble as well!"

We could go nowhere. If we weren't getting into trouble with my father, we were getting into trouble with the priests. In particular, they were at their most enthusiastic when it came to denouncing the crossroads dancing at Lismoyny. Once, when the doctor called to see whether I might take Joe's sick American wife Nancy with me, he stood in the kitchen and said coaxingly, "It will do her a power of good."

"Well it won't do me any good," I retorted. I was young, full of life and only out for a bit of fun. At the crossroads, boards were laid out flat on the dusty road for the dancers but we had been warned from the pulpit that such events were dangerous to a girl's modesty.

Equipped with a stout ashplant, our new curate Father Troy knew well where to go to catch out couples and would walk miles up dusty laneways and over ditches to find them. One evening, he prevailed upon Father Bracken to come to a reluctant decision.

"We'll go out tomorrow evening," he snapped. "Just the two of us to run them and maybe make them think twice about going out again."

"Ah, but Father,' interrupted the older priest. "What do you want to be doing the like of that for?"

Nevertheless, the two men set out the next evening for one of the most popular courting spots in the parish. Father Bracken took up position at the end of the laneway to catch any couples that the young curate might drive up from the other end. His heart wasn't in the job, but Father Troy was eager to catch someone or something in the act. It wasn't long before he made a drive at a young couple and you couldn't see their feet for dust.

Standing aside in the laneway at the other end, Father Bracken shouted: "Run quick, run quick or he'll catch ye!"

Larry, meanwhile, had so far managed to stay on the right side of the church. That was because Father McCormack needed him one September, when he sold his old town house to the Kennys and moved out to Kilcoursey. The house, which had once been a Goodbody residence, was an old building, so Larry spent some time walking around the leaded guttering and repairing the broken soffits. For months, he could be found running up ladders and in and out of chimneys like a little rat. In fact, the house was so big that it once caused an old parishioner to exclaim: "God, Father – it's far from Bethlehem you are now!"

After Larry had worked in Kilcoursey for a while, the young carpenter got to know Father McCormack's housemaid. Soon they started to go out together and one evening, he took her up to the Ballinough hills on a date. Before long, they found a spot at the end of a stonecutters' lane where there were few paths and the whole place was thick with ferns.

Unbeknownst to either, Father Troy was quickly bearing down on their position with almighty swings of his ashplant. He crept up to the spot where the couple were sitting and got ready to make his move. In one stroke, he slipped the ashplant's crook handle around the young man's collar and pulled him up. The curate got a great shock, because he didn't expect a Gaynor to be on the other end.

"I…I…can't believe this," he stammered. "Larry would you ever get up and go home!"

CHAPTER TWENTY-THREE

Stations of the Cross

One evening, when the snow was thick on the ground, I slipped out the window and followed Larry to the hall in Clara. Earlier that day, I discovered that he had arranged to meet a girl at the short dance, and I didn't want to be left out of anything. I must have slid on the bike about ten times between our house and Doorleys. It was like the Stations of the Cross. Every time I attempted to cycle, the wheels went from under me. *Now*, I said to myself, *he's gone and I won't catch up to him.*

Fortunately however, Larry was also finding the going tough, and eventually I spotted him pushing his bike through a thick bank of snow near the main road. Ducking behind the big beech tree, I decided that from then on, if Larry got off to push his bike, I would do the same. I didn't want him to see me because he would tell me to go home.

When I eventually reached River Street, I was freezing cold. Small groups of lads hung around outside the hall and as I dismounted, one of them beckoned to me. His name was Ned Stones – a lad from Aughamore that I had gone with before and he was mad to the world about me. I walked warily over the icy ground to meet him.

"How are you, Cat?" he asked, stepping from one foot to the other in an attempt to keep warm.

"Ah sure," I replied, smiling mischievously, "I'd be better if I had someone to take me to the dance."

Linking my arm in his, I walked up to the door of River Street Hall. Ned, who was delighted with his luck, fumbled in his pockets for the shilling and eight pence that would pay to admit us both but after he had handed over his ticket to the steward, I disappeared for the night, leaving him to find his own girl.

I soon spotted Larry and when the opportunity came, I strutted up to him and tapped him on the shoulder.

"Could I have the pleasure of this dance?" I asked cheekily.

His eyes widened in surprise to see me standing there instead of at home.

"You're a real hard ticket, Cat," he laughed.

All the great dancers were inside and Bill Fleming's Dance Band was first class. As we took to the floor, some people looked sourly in our direction.

"Ah, the Gaynors are here," they sighed. "We'll never get a dance now."

We were used to comments like that because we were full of music in our house. As a result, we had a great night out and were never short of good dancing partners.

I admired Patsy Egan, because the pointed toes of his shoes stood out from the hobnailed boots of the other dancers. Unfortunately, Ned and Tommie were also there, and one of them was always on the lookout to see what I was doing.

During the evening, I started to dance with a young man from Clashawaun called Bulldog Conlon. He was so nicknamed because of his looks, but I didn't want him for anything other than his great dancing.

After a small break in the music, Bill Fleming conferred with his pal Tom Johnson. Then the accordion players' decision was relayed to drummer John Slammon and the band struck up a slow waltz. We joined the other young couples on the floor:

I'll be with you in apple blossom time,
I'll be with you to change your name to mine,
One day in May, I'll come and say,
Happy is the bride the sun shines on today.

What a wonderful wedding there will be,
What a wonderful day for you and me,
Church-bells will chime, you will be mine,
In apple blossom time.

As we danced the Valletta, Ned watched us from a corner and when there was a gap in the music, he took me aside and began to question me angrily.

"Kathleen," he asked. "How did you get in with Bulldog Conlon?"

I was disgusted because I could go nowhere without someone watching me.

Ned needn't have worried because the next dance was a 'choice dance', and another lad cut in on the Bulldog. I was disappointed because my new partner had two left feet and I hated to dance with anybody who couldn't keep time. '*One, two, three, come balance with me*,' went the rhyme. '*When the right foot is crazy, the left foot is lazy; don't be un-aisy, I'll teach you to waltz.*'

Despite the snow, I had managed to cycle to the dance, but when it ended at one o'clock I had no one to bring me home. Larry had gone on to join the card school that started in the corner and Ned and Tommie were nowhere to be found. As everybody began to trickle out of the hall into the cold night air, I saw a man I knew leaning on a bike and he beckoned me over. Cupping a match in one hand to light a cigarette, he told me he was coming my way, so I decided to go with him. Although he was married, I knew that he had an awful reputation of being an oul' ram, but he behaved like a perfect gentleman all the way home. Soon we passed Mrs Molloy's school and were making our way past Kilmucklin.

When I got to the gate, Larry was standing there with a grin on his face and I couldn't figure out how he had got there before me.

"You must have hit the road in spots," I said.

"In the name of Christ," he laughed. "How did you get in with that fella?"

As we chatted there, we both agreed that there was no sense in the two of us walking into the house, since my father would almost certainly catch us. Instead, I stayed outside for a while, smoked a Player's and waited for Larry to get ready for bed.

After about fifteen minutes, I lifted the latch and began to creep across the kitchen. I never noticed my father standing there until the match had been struck. The glow was enough to light up the settle bed and with an air of imperious triumph, he cried: "*Aha!* You should be ashamed of yourself. Look at all your brothers!"

"Well, feck them," I muttered under my breath.

I was sure that I could see Lar half-opening one eye to see what was going on. After threatening to have words with me the next morning, he blew the match out and returned to bed.

When he had gone, I opened the bedroom door and peered in at the lads in the settle bed. In bitter humour, I decided to christen them after a play that was on in Clara that week. The main characters were oul' men who never went with women and never did anything wrong, so it seemed very appropriate somehow.

"Hah-hah, how's the Gasun Conroys?" I hissed and the bed shook with silent laughter.

CHAPTER TWENTY-FOUR

Kilmucklin

Whirling a track hammer in his right hand, my father swiped the embankment grass as he passed. As he walked, he half-hummed, half-sang a favourite tune:

> *The signal for starting I heard but in vain,*
> *Not a glimpse could I see of her; the train without started*
> *The charming young wida' I met on the train.*

"God, Mr Gaynor must be a Permanent Way Ganger again!" exclaimed Kathleen Fox.

As if in answer, came another burst of song through the open window – '…*'twas no child at all, it was only a dowdy.*' Kathleen – who had first recognised my father's brown boots before she saw the rest of him – was sure that he had gone back to his old job.

Later that day, my mother confirmed to Mrs Fox that her husband had indeed come home from Swindford where he had provided three weeks' holiday cover. Working for a daily rate of three shillings and sixpence, he was every inch the Assistant Inspector – even down to a pair of polished black shoes – and he took free lodgings with the McKeowns. But the most surprising news for the Foxes by far concerned the retirement notice that had awaited his return.

That evening, he folded the paper in half and stood gravely in front of the ramblers.

"Well, lads, unless ye like your kitchen under new management, ye'll all be finding a new fire soon enough," he announced.

"Are you raving or what?" cried oul' Ned Robbins, eyeing my father as if he were mad.

"Ah hould your gallop," answered Colm Fox. "Isn't he talking about retiring? Sure none of his own become milesmen."

It was true enough. Although Joe was a fireman and Tommie and Ned worked at the station, these jobs did not entitle them to keep the house. My father smiled as he recalled how Tommie, on his first morning, had instructions to meet John Sheridan at half past eight in the station.

But his son, who had one leg up on the stool to tie his bootlaces, answered back sulkily: "I'm not going to that job at all. That's only an oul' turnip stalk job."

He had the strangest sayings but loved the work afterwards.

"So anyway," my father said. "I'm after getting a letter from Kingsbridge wishing me luck, so I may make me own arrangements. I've lived in this house for over sixty years, but sure there's no point getting bothered stupid about it. You get your notice to quit from the company and that's that – unless of course you were a widow woman in it. *Then* you might get a chance. I should've been born a widow, for all the good working done me."

Of course, we all agreed that we would have been stuck only for the fact that through my mother, we owned a few fields in Kilmucklin. One of the main alterations would be an addition built on as a bedroom for the lads so that they didn't have to sleep in the kitchen any more. Since we weren't expecting electricity lines any time soon, my mother was prepared to cook in the same way that she had always done.

In the early stages, all the lads helped to dig the foundations, but it was my father who took command of the job. The men worked there every evening after six o'clock. Tommie drew the sand from Jenny's field with the pony and cart and was charged with the job of mixing concrete. Larry, who was only thirteen and still in school, was a great help because he knew a lot about geometry.

When my father realised that the foundations would be over two metres deep before they hit *terra firma*, he looked for timber to use as shuttering. Without it, there was a danger that the earthen walls might cave in. Fortunately, a local builder named Barney Duffy had been hired to tear down an old granary near Clara Station, and he gave him some of the old wood.

Eventually however, the heavy lifting took its toll and when his back got sore, my father was forced to take it easy for a while. One evening, while my mother made barley water as a cure, he went rummaging in the bedroom.

"Come on and have a look at this oul' foram," he called as he crouched on bended knee.

Drying her hands on her *praiscín*, my mother hurried in and together the couple sat on the bed to peer at the yellowed and frayed GS&WR parchment in my father's lap. Running a rough finger along the paper, he read the words aloud with quiet acceptance:

And in case the said Thomas Gaynor shall quit or be discharged from the service of the said Company, he hereby further agrees that he will, immediately thereupon, yield and deliver up to the said Company the keys of the gates at said level crossing, and also the full possession of said house and premises.

"Arra, we'll be grand," my mother said reassuringly. "Sure we'll have a pension of twelve shillings a week as well as all the lads out working. Thank God for what we have and that we're able to move."

My father agreed.

After the walls had been built, the house stood unfinished without its roof. The beginning of 1933 was brutal, with the blizzard persisting in many places until May and Kilmucklin was not spared. Snow and sleet spattered down the flue and onto the cold hearth but the poured concrete chimney was safe from serious weather damage.

Then, towards the end of that year, my father had to give the project serious consideration once again. Since he was due to retire before the following summer, he decided to seek the advice of a carpenter called Dick Recks, to whom Larry was now apprenticed.

That Friday, when Dick came out to the house my mother, wanting to be polite, showed him into the parlour room.

"I'll get Larry for you now Mr Recks," she said as she closed the door.

When I went to look for Larry, he was out at the sheds.

"In the name of all that's holy, where did your man go?" he asked.

"Oh, he's in the parlour room freezing to death," I replied with a wry look on my face. The parlour was always a cold barracks of a room and my mother in her eagerness might as well have sent him into a fridge.

Meanwhile, my father had returned home and was already talking to the carpenter. It turned out that Dick was very busy.

"I can start tomorrow," he sighed, "but I'll have to fit ye in about five o'clock in the morning."

The next morning, they set off for Kilmucklin in the carpenter's van, having loaded it first with ladders, Larry's bike and a box of tools. They stayed there working on the roof until the afternoon when the weather turned bad. Larry waited on his own for a while because my father had left earlier, promising to return.

An hour passed and the sky got greyer. Down came big, greasy drops of rain, plopping onto the new windows and making a muddy heap out of the sand left over from the building work. After a few minutes, there was a gap in the weather, but with no sign of my father coming Larry cleaned up and got ready to come home. On the way out, he remembered to take the tin bucket because my mother needed it to milk the cows.

Whistling, he balanced the bucket on his handlebars, but had scarcely left the building site when it began to rain again. As heavy drops pelted the road, he searched frantically for something to keep himself dry but finding that the only thing to hand was the tin bucket, he stuck it on his head and brought the handle down over his face like a chin strap. Now he could hear the rain hitting off the bucket, but he couldn't see or hear anything.

At the same time that Larry was making for the Tullamore Road, milkman John Robbins was struggling up the hill at Berrigan's Corner with his pony and trap. Lar never saw the cart coming, because if you have a bucket on your head and you're going like a sonny, you wouldn't either. In the nick of time, he swerved, water still belting off the bucket, and narrowly avoided going into the dike. We looked at the wheel tracks afterwards and could see how lucky his escape had been.

When the interior of the house was finished, Larry brought different coloured slabs out of a nearby chapel and made a path out of them at the back of the house. Afterwards when Ned Robbins came in, he said, 'I'll go round be the Vestry' because it reminded him of a church. Altogether, the work had taken about four years but when it was finished, the new house nestled snugly in a field adjacent to the Burkes' stone house in Kilmucklin.

On the ninth of April 1934 – the day after my twentieth birthday – Mr Morton wrote from Kingsbridge Station to a colleague, advising him that my father was ready to give up possession. The tenancy was to be transferred rent free to Jim Lennon, providing he agreed to take responsibility for the crossing gates.

It was a fine Tuesday in May when we finally began to shift furniture from Ashfield and the lane was a white carpet of cow parsley. The early start – a concession to the pony who might be bothered by flies later in the day – saw the lads pile the car high with delph, the big goose dish, the press bed and the kitchen table.

My father had cautioned the lads to be careful in handling the pony, since it was an unpredictable animal. A couple of weeks before the move, he and Ned had taken it to the fair in Tullamore where they bought a pig and tied it in a creel at the back of the car. Straddled either side of their purchase, they set off for home. Suddenly and without warning, the pony bolted and it was with great difficulty that my father managed to rein it in.

Later that morning, Larry and Bab's brother-in-law Tom Feehan were coming back down to the railway house to collect furniture. I had been over in Kilmucklin and was cycling back to collect my mother's bits and pieces to put into the car for them.

I had to go out onto the main road for about a quarter of a mile and was just coming to the top of the laneway when I saw the two lads trotting towards me. I stood in to let them by but they wouldn't pass and kept chucking the pony out of divilment. If I tried to go left, they laughed and pulled the pony left. If I made a move to the right, they chucked the reins and blocked me on that side too.

Suddenly the pony, annoyed by the constant pulling at its head, reared the same as if there was no cart under it. There were two shafts either side but the animal acted the very same as if it was out in the field. Putting its grey forelegs to the ceiling, it bolted and I could feel a gush of wind as it passed.

"Oh God!" Larry shouted. "Cat's killed altogether!"

They started to gallop towards the hill and I knew that if they got out on the main road they were all finished. Thankfully however, the effort of pulling the cart up the incline was too much for the pony and they all came to a stop at the top of the lane.

A couple of days later, a tinker came down the lane selling oil-cloth. Having heard about the incident on the hill, my father swapped our grey pony for the small and docile animal that the tinker owned. The Lord only knows what he told him in order to make the trade.

On the heel of the evening, Ned and Larry went to meet the Lennons to help them settle in. Jim Lennon, who had no children, was a platelayer assigned to that section of line until his retirement and he was very enthusiastic about getting the house. The windows and doors of Ashfield were in need of painting both inside and outside, but Jim had volunteered to do all the work by himself, at a cost of about six shillings to the railway for buying the paint. It would have cost the company a pound otherwise.

When my brothers eventually got him as far as Ashfield, they had to take his boots off and help him into bed. The poor man had gone out and got drunk on the strength of his good fortune. After that, they muffled the warm embers of the hearth, closed the door on the railway house for the last time and set out in the dark for Kilmucklin.

CHAPTER TWENTY-FIVE

Oul' Jackeen Feehan

About a month before we moved to the new house, Bab was married in Durrow by Father Gerald Cooney and had her wedding breakfast in the parlour room in Ashfield. The priest was invited back afterwards for the fine spread that my mother had prepared. Using three bakers, each slightly smaller than the next, Julia Fox from Tara had baked the wedding cake on her own hearth at home. We finished off the icing, and it was quite an achievement in the end because it tasted just as if it were shop-bought.

Once we had eaten, my father took out the accordion and we had a couple of dances on the stone floor. When Julia Fox took the floor she kicked her heels to a solo dance, to which my father played a reel called 'The Blackberry Blossom'. After that, we danced a couple of half-sets. The cake had pride of place on the table but as I began to step nearer to it, the top tier shook unsteadily.

"Oh Lord!" my mother cried, raising her hands to her face. "That one is going to knock that cake down."

Of course, once I heard that, being full of divilment, I danced even harder.

Then a glass of whiskey was pressed into Bab's hand and she was encouraged to give a rendition of her favourite ballad, the refrain of which was *'Auctioneer, Auctioneer, won't you cry off the sale'*. Told through the voice of a sibling, it concerned the declining fortunes of an Irish family who was upon the verge of giving up their home to the sheriff, but was saved by the return of a long-lost son from America:

> *Now the very best bidder was a man quite unknown,*
> *He paid down his money and he purchased our home.*
> *Then the stranger stepped forward saying*
> *'Your sorrow is o'er,*
> *I've returned you your home; I'm your long-lost son.'*
>
> *What joy and rejoicement was felt on that day,*
> *When my brother embraced his mother so grey,*
> *And his poor sickly sister so deathly and pale,*
> *And that put an end to the good sheriff's sale.*

My father meanwhile had received various reports in Durrow church that morning from neighbours who knew Jack Feehan's mother. One man told him that she was of 'a fighting breed'. Another said that she was 'a rale oul' rough country wan'. The more stories he heard like that, the more he was inclined to think that things wouldn't work out for his daughter. He didn't have anything personal against Bab's mother-in-law, but he understood that there would be too many of them in it for comfort.

Afterwards, he asked Father Cooney if he would like to see the new house and the priest said he would, so the two men drove up to Kilmucklin and spent an hour up there. After that, the newly-weds went to Dublin on their honeymoon and we thought that was great. They were going to America in our eyes. There was great excitement, but shortly after the wedding was over we were finished in that house.

When Bab came home, a gang of us went out to tea in the Derries with the aim of becoming acquainted with the old woman of the house. As we sat around the table, the original Mrs Feehan eyed us carefully and you could cut the silence with a knife. As she sat there, Bab looked every inch the lovely young bride whereas her mother-in-law, who was more old-fashioned, sat in her *praiscín* apron and hob-nailed boots. Eventually her gaze settled on me.

"And who are you?" she asked.

"I'm Jack's new wife," I replied gravely and shook her hand.

I was very wild and full of mischief, whereas Bab had a different nature. Like her mother, she was very gentle, but Mrs Feehan was a strong character who spoke her mind.

Once, during a visit, I went out with her to get a bucket of spuds and as we hunched down beside the pit, she enquired whether Bab was sick at home often. Taking care not to take the lazy way out by getting the potatoes from the edge of the scraw, I replied that I didn't think so.

All this time, Bab, who was ill with morning sickness, had been watching us from the little window and when I came inside, she called me into the room.

"What was she saying to you?" she asked.

I sat on the end of the bed and looked at her quizzically.

"What are you asking me that for?" I replied.

I was beginning to wonder whether something was going on and if the stories my father had heard were true. I had an idea that the mother-in-law had it in for Bab and didn't want to worry her, but she was insistent.

"That oul' wan," she pressed. "Was she saying anything to you?"

"She asked me were you delicate?" I said.

With that, Bab sat back in the bed and closed her eyes in resignation. I couldn't understand why she was so curious about what her mother-in-law had said but I soon found out.

Standing in the kitchen was a dresser with a hanging shelf. The shelf was used for cups, some of which had been a wedding present for the new couple. Others had *'A Present from Dundalk'* written on the side with nicely shaped handles that Bab admired. That gave her mother-in-law a great brainwave.

When Jack arrived home one evening, the first thing he noticed was the empty hanger shelf. Next, his eyes lit on his mother, who was sitting looking at it with her arms folded.

"Well, ye may blame yer new wife for that," she said stoutly, nodding towards the bare wood.

"But sure what would Bab want with cups?" Jack asked.

Shortly after that, I cycled out for a visit and as Bab poured my tea, she told me the latest news.

"That oul' wan is after letting on it was me that took the cups and brought them home, but sure Mam has delph of her own."

I smiled because I could see the funny side. We bought all our crockery from a Dublin dealer who went from door to door in a pony and cart selling it out of an old-fashioned straw basket, and I knew that Bab had paid no heed to the cups on the hanging shelf except for those she had received as presents.

"When Jack and the neighbours kicked the boards out of the way to clane the well outside the door, weren't all the cups sitting in the bucket," Bab explained.

"Ah, do you know what I'd have done with her?" I chuckled. "I'd have put her down in the well after the cups. I'd have her heels up and her head down."

"It's all right for you Cahy,' she chuckled. "You haven't to live in it."

Of course, it would be pointless to say that we bore a grudge against the old woman. She really was the funniest character who ever lived in that part of the world, and we wondered what she would do next. We didn't have to wait long to find out.

One wet, dreary day, Jack was working on the roads and was due in at half five. In those days, roadmen wearing goggles used to break stones to fill holes with and even though there were no machines, it was the best job they ever had. I often cycled past on my way into town and the men would stay all day chatting to you over a shovel.

Whilst Jack was out working, his mother went into the bedroom. With disbelief, Bab watched as she heaved the fibre mattress off the bed and slumped it onto the stone floor of the kitchen. After a few moments, she wrestled it through the front door and dragged it behind her down the muddy lane. Bab couldn't make head nor tail of what she was at until she got halfway between Minnocks and Feehans, put the mattress under a bush and lay down on it.

As the rain began to soak her, she started to shout: "Jackeen Feehan's after putting me out…he put me, out so he did!"

The Minnocks heard her as they passed with cars coming from town and from the bog.

"Oh, wait till I tell you!" one of them cried when he arrived home. "Ah the oul' Feehan wan's gone in the head altogether now. Do you know where she is? She's in the rain. What'll we do? Will we go out and bring her in?"

"Oh Jaysus you won't," said Mrs Minnock. "The dinner's on. Pack yerselves childer, and lave her alone to get wet."

When Jack came home and saw the bare springs of his mother's bed, he scratched his head.

"Where's the mattress?" he asked.

"Your mother's after dragging it out the door," said Bab. "Ah the poor oul' cratur, Jack," she said kindly. "You better go and bring her in. Sure she'll get all wet."

CHAPTER TWENTY-SIX

A Fireman's Girl

"I don't know where we're going to put the woman," my mother cried, throwing her hands up in despair.

My father's answer was blunt.

"Well she doesn't have to stop here if she doesn't want to," he replied.

The source of the argument lay on the table – a letter from Aunt Katie. Annoyed with my father because he never left her enough money to buy proper bedclothes, my mother leaned her floury elbows on the table edge and looked gloomily at the envelope. Out of a sense of propriety, she wanted to ensure that her sister-in-law would be well looked after during her stay.

After Uncle Larry died, Aunt Katie had been given work at Kilkenny Station as a means of keeping her home. Every day, she sat in the waiting room, ensuring that anyone who needed to use the facilities paid the shilling fee and when all the passengers had gone, she tidied up and lit a fire in the little grate. When all was as it should be, she could take out her book and read for a while.

Since I knew that this would be Katie's last official holiday before retiring the following December, I set off for town to buy messages. I was also on the lookout for something that would persuade her to let me down to Bagenalstown for a week.

Soon I reached the corner of Main Street and made straight for D.E. Williams which had a grocery and paper shop adjoining. As usual, I left my bike outside, safe in the knowledge that it would still be there when I came out.

"Well how are you?" asked the manager, Sean Kelly.

"Grand," I replied. "I have an oul' aunt coming to stay, so I'm trying to get the house readied out."

While we spoke, Eileen O'Halloran pottered away in the background, adjusting stock and dusting shelves, but when she got the chance she gave me a knowing wink. Sean had come in for his usual daytime drink and she was reminding me to wait until his half-hour was up.

Once he had gone, Miss O'Halloran, wearing her white jacket with the D.E. Williams logo on the top pocket, moved a small stepladder into position in front of one of the glass cabinets. Then, taking care not to knock down any of the smaller bottles lined up at the front, she lifted out a bottle of port wine and emptied some of its contents into two glasses. When she was ready, the two of us stood in behind an advertisement of a girl selling Sweet Afton cigarettes so that we couldn't be seen.

"Well Cat, do you think I have much of a chance?" she eventually asked.

"Oh Lord, I'm putting in a woeful word for you at home," I replied, gulping a mouthful of wine. "And you know that Tommie is real solid as well, so you can't go wrong there."

My glass was empty.

'Well I think he's a lovely chap,' the matronly shop assistant said. Nodding vigorously, I reached for the half-empty bottle.

From time to time, Miss O'Halloran, her cheeks reddened by the wine, would go out to attend to a customer at the wooden-panelled counter. Once I heard her say "Thank you very much," I knew that we could get on with our sampling.

Outside, the day turned dull and the rain began to come down in sheets. As we stood there, I suddenly realised that I was well overdue with the messages.

"Oh God, I better go home before Tommie comes," I said anxiously, because I knew that he was sure to stop in on his way home from the station to buy the *Independent* for my father.

In a panic, I cycled off; my head spinning with wine. Hearing the sound of Tommie's bike behind me, the curiosity got the better of me, so I turned to look back. I could picture him saying in his usual solid way, "Good evening Eileen".

There were messages each side of my bike and the handlebars wobbled with the weight. Suddenly, I was thrown off balance and the handlebars twisted around. The wheel skidded and down I flopped into the mud with my good leather coat on me. That's what I got for my curiosity!

CHAPTER TWENTY-SEVEN

The Humours of Kilkenny

When my father called me at first light the next morning to rake the hearth, I leant over the side of the bed and clattered my boots on the floor to pretend I was up. At midday, my mother rose and I dressed her in front of the fire. Once I had brushed her hair, I helped to fit her truss – a support for her collapsed womb and a consequence of having eight children. I smiled as I remembered the party we had at home while they were above in Fannins of Dublin getting it fitted.

Feeling as though I needed a holiday myself, I chose my moment carefully.

"Mam," I said, as I adjusted the straps. "Is there any chance that I could g'off down to Kilkenny to help Katie when she's going back?"

I knew it was a lot to ask, since my mother might struggle on her own. As usual however, she was more concerned for my welfare than she was for her own.

"God, sure it's not fair,' she cried. "All them lads'll marry and you'll be stuck here an oul' maid. Ye should be enjoying yourself," she said.

Of course, by the time I saw my cousins standing on the platform in Bagenalstown, any notion of help had flown out of my head and I wondered what divilment I could get up to. Amidst the billowing engine smoke, Aunt Katie and I were crowded by Bridie, Kathleen, Nellie and Mary. The older girls, who were living in England, had come home on holidays and after hugging, we trudged out of the station with our bags and began the slow climb up the hill. The house itself stood in the distance – a semi-detached building with smoke rising from a single chimney into the late summer sky.

As we filed over the little stone bridge, a single motor passed, raising dust on its way to the station. Soon we were strolling past the long hedge which ran down the length of the front garden. It afforded the house some privacy from the main road, and since I had been there last, Aunt Katie had been busy with a rockery and a bed of flowers.

Everything about Bagenalstown was so different from our own home in Kilmucklin. Bounded on one side by a branch line that ran to Borris-in-Ossory, the Gaynors' home was much grander than ours. I was struck in particular by the chequered black and white tiles in the hallway, the big dining room and the high ceilings. The hall opened out into a wide reception area, off which a grand staircase rose to the right. In the kitchen, there was a nice country table, two china cabinets, a wood-fired stove and a fender that read '*Home Sweet Home*'. There was even a scullery off the kitchen where the girls did the washing up.

Suddenly I was broken out of my reverie by Nellie. She was a tall girl, thinner than me, with brown hair and eyes. Amongst all my cousins, I got on with her the best.

"Did I tell you that I wanted to take the train to Kilkenny tomorrow?" she asked. "I was thinking of going shopping and sure if I don't see anything, what harm is a couple of hours gallavanting?"

Impulsively, I blurted out: "I'll go with you."

"Jaysus," she said, grabbing my hand excitedly. "The two of us will go!"

Early the following morning, we stood in Bagenalstown station and apart from the men in the green-painted signal cabin, there were few people about. The house had been busy during the night, with a fireman and then a driver being woken by the station porter for their trains. I yawned sleepily until a shrill whistle broke my daze, and I looked up to see our train as it passed Aunt Katie's house.

As we sat into the carriage, we smiled at each other in anticipation of a good day out.

"Mam says that your mother is not too well," Nellie said demurely.

"Ah, God love her," I replied. "She wouldn't see me without a holiday."

"But what about your father?" she probed.

"Ah, I don't want to think about him today," I replied.

Nellie had been the apple of her own father's eye. As a child, she used to comb his hair and take him a drink before bed, but I never had that kind of relationship. In fact, it was just the opposite.

Just before leaving for Kilkenny, my father had shaken me by the shoulders, shouting: "You'll mind your mother whether you like it or not."

"She's your wife," I retorted. "You mind her!"

A comfortable silent reigned for a time, broken only by the sound of the train clicking over the points, and I gazed vacantly at the countryside as it galloped past the window.

When we reached Kilkenny, the station was full of Thursday morning shoppers. As we stepped down from the carriage, Nellie spotted a passenger train standing at the opposite platform. I followed her gaze and looked to see a fireman dressed in overalls and cap chatting off the footplate to a station porter.

"Oh God, Kathleen," she squealed excitedly. "There's a fella I used to go with!"

Despite his half-hearted salute, she went running over the bridge to meet him and I trotted behind.

"Are you not going to say hello?" she asked breathlessly.

The man didn't respond. Instead, he tapped the engine's quarter glass with a finger and spoke casually without turning.

"You never told me you were married," he quipped. "So I saw your mother and had to get the news second-hand."

"Ah forget about that now and come here," Nellie beamed. "I have another Gaynor for you. This is Dinny Houlihan," she said, ushering me forward.

Carefully wiping the grime from his hands with a cloth rag, the fireman looked me up and down.

"And does this other Gaynor have a name?" he smiled, relaxing his scowl.

"My name's Polly," I answered gravely.

He thrust his hand down from the footplate to shake mine.

"Well Polly, I'm glad to meet you," he said.

"Jaysus, Kathleen,' giggled Nellie under her breath, "you're fierce. You're getting worse!'

At forty, the fireman was a man at the latter end of his youth but he was fresh-faced and full of life and, despite the fact that he was working on an engine, I couldn't help noticing how well-presented he was. The subject of Aunt Katie's secretive conversation suddenly became clear. The previous night, she had spoken to Nellie about someone we would most likely meet in Kilkenny, and cautioned her not to ignore him.

"I'm staying above in Bagenalstown with my Aunt," I explained, glancing sideways at Nellie. "And this girl here is a first cousin of mine."

"Begod," Dinny exclaimed, swinging onto the platform. "So how long are you staying?"

"A whole week or maybe more," I answered. "I only come yesterday."

"Oh, the Purcells are holding a dance at their house in a couple of days' time," Nellie said effusively. "You should come."

A rather more bemused fireman stepped back onto the footplate.

"Well, Nellie," he said. "Do you mind if I come out tomorrow evening? I think I'll take a holiday."

"You'd be more than welcome," she said.

Afterwards, over a cup of tea, Nellie smiled indulgently.

"You really are fierce, you know. Imagine calling yourself Polly. You'll have to tell him tomorrow."

She gave my hand a playful squeeze but I just smiled wickedly.

"How do you know him anyhow?" I asked.

"Well," she began. "Dinny used to come to stay at our house with two other men, when he worked as a fireman on the Ballywilliam train. I was doing most of the cooking that time because Mam had to go to work every day in Kilkenny. I started doing a line with him, but now he's put out over me not telling him that I got married."

Nellie paused to take another draw of tea from the steaming pot in front of us. Taking a quick mouthful, she continued:

'Do you know, that man is awful lucky. A few years ago, he slipped coming off a train in Kilkenny station and broke his hip. It didn't happen only of a very frosty morning, and he was brought to Dr Steeven's Hospital and then convalesced with us for a few months."

"But he's back working now?" I probed.

"Oh yes," she replied. "You see, the G.S.R. had been paying Dinny full wages all along but eventually they asked him to choose between either a lump sum or light work on the railway. But when he wrote to his mother in Portlaoise, she put her foot down and told him not to take any lump sum. She knew Dinny wasn't a man for hoarding and would blow it in no time. Where would that leave him then?

"Go back and get light work," she told him.

On Friday evening, Dinny came out to Aunt Katie's house. He stood politely on the step until I answered the door and invited him in.

"You look grand," I said by way of compliment.

"Oh begod aye, I'm a woeful spatter altogether," he laughed, pausing to adjust his tie in the mirror.

The table was set in the dining room, the bay window of which looked out onto the fruit trees in the garden. Evening sunlight streamed onto the linen tablecloth and we all looked forward to a nice tea, the bulk of which the girls had helped their mother to prepare. Sitting in the green-belted summer dress I had bought in Kilkenny, I felt made up altogether.

Soon, we were all eating heartily. I looked at Dinny's well-ironed shirt and slightly receding, neatly combed hair and wondered what 'light work' he was supposed to be doing, because I had seen him up on the footplate. He could easily have been dressed for his own wedding. If there was any awkwardness left between him and Nellie, I couldn't see it.

Mixing sweet and savoury with seeming indifference, I watched as he ate a sandwich, immediately followed by a scone with a bit of jam and was now loading his plate with a slice of ham and tomato. Suddenly, his voice cut across my daydream.

"Would you ever pass the salt, Polly?" he asked.

I looked at the fireman strangely until, with a smile, I remembered how I had introduced myself the previous day. It was just so unbelievable that he couldn't see how I was codding him. When

Michael, the chapel clerk, went into the hall to laugh, I struggled to keep a straight face.

When we were finished, he thanked my aunt for the tea, excused himself and said, "I think myself and Polly will go for a walk."

Katie looked up from her plate sharply.

"Give that up," she snapped, her blue eyes fixing on him with a piercing stare. "What are you saying; Pollying out of ye?"

Without warning, the laughter I had been holding in all through tea erupted in a fit of giggles, and I almost fell off my chair. Aunt Katie knew then of course that I was the cause of all the confusion, so she lit on me and had a word about bringing Dinny up the garden path.

"How dare you," she said, giving me a severe look. "Dinny, her name is Kathleen."

He said nothing for a moment but then took a good-humoured fit of laughing.

That Saturday, we all danced out the road to Purcells. The Gaynors were very great with the family, and a dinner was to be given in honour of me because I was the visitor. We arrived to find a table set in the kitchen with lovely scones out of a big fire on the hearth. Soon, the house filled with musicians, neighbours and friends and the dance was so big that at the interval, the guests had to have their tea in sessions. When ten had finished at the table, ten more would come in to take their place.

Sometimes it was hard to get Dinny all to myself, because a lot of people besides the Gaynors knew him. That was on account of him being very popular in the dancehalls of Bagenalstown and he had an awful lot of mates – anyone who drinks always will.

Once, he took a local girl to a dance, but she slipped during a set and injured her leg. One young man volunteered to run to the girl's house to wake up her parents, while another was sent for the doctor. By the time the doctor got there, the music had stopped and a large crowd had gathered on the dance floor. Elbowing his way into the middle, he knelt down to treat the girl.

"God dammit," he shouted. "Will you give her some space. Can't you see that she needs air?"

So the crowd parted and he opened his bag. As he began to check her leg, various people volunteered their advice from the floor.

"Rubber heels," one young man said knowingly, and the onlookers nodded their heads in agreement. But the doctor, who had misheard turned sharply.

"*Ah, rub her arse*," he snapped. "Isn't it her leg that's broke?"

It was almost two in the morning before the entertainment in Purcells' wound to a close and Frank Smith, who sang 'Song of Songs', was clapped on the back. As they left, some of the neighbours gave the promise of a return the following week and waved to us as they cycled past.

CHAPTER TWENTY-EIGHT

The Abbey Players

After a few months had passed, I decided that Dinny should meet my father and mother, so I wrote and asked him to come and visit. A few days later, Peter Flattery, our postman, came out with the mail from High Street and when he had handed it over, he took off his cap and bag and sat down to have a cup of tea. After a while, I suspected by the way he was hovering around me like an oul' cock that he was waiting to give me something. Eventually, he withdrew a wire from his pocket.

Now in those days, a wire coming to a house always meant a death or something sudden so naturally my parents were quite anxious. Each believing it to be for them, neither wanted to be the first to open it, but when my father realised who it was from, he saw red.

"Jaysus Christ," he shouted. "Will you stop that fella from sending wires!"

Eagerly, I plucked the envelope from his outstretched hand and took it into the parlour where Larry sat listening to the gramophone. Tearing it open, I read the following: '*Hope you are in good foram*'.

"Oh God damn it," I winked to Lar. "This is from *foram*!"

'Well come on,' he said impatiently. 'What else does it say?'

I took a second glance at the wire. 'He's only sending it to make an appointment. It says nothing only '*...meeting...Tullamore... Denis...half two...Sunday.*'

The next day, I set about arranging accommodation for Dinny

in Williams' hotel and, I was delighted until my mother brought me back to reality.

"What are you going to do about your father?" she asked.

"I don't know," I replied. "But whatever happens, we can harl'y leave him at the hotel."

"Well alright," she said. "In that case, we'll have to run him out to the house."

So, on Sunday afternoon, she waved out the window as I cycled off in my new tweed jacket and skirt. By the time I met Dinny on the road halfway between Clara and Tullamore, he had cycled twenty miles from Portlaoise, having borrowed the bicycle from his County Council pal.

Before we sat down, he opened a little leather bag, inside which was a set of raingear and a cloth cap. It had rained the night before so he spread the raingear out on the grass.

"Well this is grand," he said.

"Now don't forget what we talked about," I reminded him. "My father is to have no idea we even know one another."

Later, we went into Tullamore and had our dinner and tea in Hayes' hotel. As we sat in the snug afterwards with our pint of stout and glass of brandy, Dinny suddenly stood up.

"Ah Christ," he cried, "I'm after leaving all my raingear behind!"

We went back and searched everywhere but to no avail.

Meanwhile, my mother was doing her best to lie about where I was, because my father would see red if he found out the truth. As the afternoon drew on, he looked at his pocket watch every few minutes.

"Where is she now?" he muttered. "Ah sure, Kathleen's minding the house for Joe," my mother replied.

That was believable because Joe was living in Clara and his wife Nancy was very ill.

At half five that evening Ned, who knew Dinny from Bagenalstown, took the pony and trap out of the station yard and clipped down the hill towards the hotel. I had cautioned Dinny to remove any jewellery that he was wearing since my father, who didn't approve of such things, didn't even wear a wedding band. So with rings and all shoved well into his pockets, Dinny sat up on the trap outside Williams' hotel and the two men set off.

I paced nervously in the parlour room until I heard a rattle of wheels in the lane. Then I reminded myself that we were to act like complete strangers, took a deep breath and walked out of the bedroom.

"This is my sister," Ned explained to Dinny. "I'm pleased to meet you," he said politely.

I was sure that we were all fit for the Abbey stage.

Conversation at tea was awkward and after some small talk about the weather, the conversation lapsed into uncomfortable silence, broken only by the clink of cutlery on delph. After a long interval, my father spoke.

"How long are you with the G.S.R.?"

"Well Mr Gaynor, it must be going on seventeen years."

"So you must be near enough to being a driver be now," my father concluded, wiping his mouth with the edge of the tablecloth.

Knowing that Dinny had failed the test, I longed for a change of subject. My mother was the only one to notice my sudden lack of appetite.

"I suppose you're going to play with that now?" she said pointedly. When my father wasn't looking, I threw her an angry glance.

But Fatty Arbuckle just ignored my dirty looks and went on eating.

"How's your mother?" she enquired suddenly, rising to fetch

the boiling kettle.

"Ah, she's bedridden Mrs Gaynor," said Dinny. "So we can only l'ave it to the man above." Then, rolling up his shirt sleeves, he enthused: "But we'd be lost only for my sister minding her."

Rising to help my mother with the teapot, I knew how his sister felt.

Later that night, I heard a chat going on in the next room and sitting bolt upright, pressed my ear to the wall. Faintly, I heard my father say: "Did you cop anything there tonight?"

"No," replied my mother. "What are you talking about?"

"Do you not see what's happening?" asked my father. "Sure, that one knew him real well, and then let on to shake hands with 'I'm pleased to meet you' and all the rest of it. She was out with him."

There was silence before my mother spoke again.

"I'm not so sure."

"You're a very harmless woman."

"Well I see nothing wrong with him."

With a creak of bedsprings, my father turned to face my mother.

"Neither do I. If she gets him she'll be doing alright. He's a lovely man, but men like that have a port in every storm. They're railway men and when they're going from Kingsbridge to Athlone they have a girl at all the stations down along. I know it because I'm looking at it. She's alright," he said, finally turning over. "But is *he* alright?"

My father didn't trust Dinny because railwaymen had an awful name, especially train drivers – who were known for taking up with girls at the station. On some evenings, without looking up from the paper, he would ask Tommie about the men who had come in with the Goods train and would get the answer: 'Gibneys'.' For both men, that was enough said.

I knew Dinny wasn't that sort of man, but he did enjoy his

drink. Before setting off from Kingsbridge on the Athlone run, he liked to put a sup of porter into a jug, which he shared with the driver Mick Gavin.

One afternoon, Tommie was on the lookout for his train coming in, because I had asked him to see if there was a letter for me. He never liked drink, was solid as a rock and to his credit was also very honest. Despite the fact that I was his own sister, he always asked me for my ticket if I was going anywhere!

From his position at the front of the train, Dinny could see Tommie marching down the platform, closing the carriage doors. As he closed each one, he made sure to give it a good slap with a shout of 'All aboard!' Dinny understood his temperament, and was cute enough to try and keep the jug out of sight until they were well clear of the station. He could manage that easily enough, but since he had a letter for me, he had to get fairly close to Tommie to give it to him. That was the difficult part. If Tommie got the smell of drink, he would give out to me, so in an effort to seem busy with the engine, Dinny turned his back and made a job of unloading the clinker onto the track.

Tommie reached the footplate just in time to hear the hot ashes hissing onto the sleepers below. Without turning, Dinny fished the letter from his pilot coat pocket and waved it aloft. Keeping one hand firmly on the raker, he felt a brisk hand remove it. Then, as the footsteps retreated down the platform and the 'all clear' was given, he breathed a sigh of relief.

Unfortunately for Dinny, it didn't matter which way he turned, because Tommie always got the smell of drink. Hanging up his coat inside the door that evening, he turned and said:

"Now I'm going to give you a tip. Don't come to me when it all goes wrong, because that fella *is* and *will be* a drunkard. He wants nothing else, only give him plenty of porter."

"What are you talking about?" I asked.

"He was on that platform today," Tommie replied. "And he was footless."

I knew that Dinny wasn't footless at all; he was just enjoying life to the full, and I was delighted to read the letter because he wanted to make a date for Sunday week.

"Wait a minute," I laughed. "I didn't get married at all yet."

"I'm only telling you," Tommie quipped, "because you're heading in that direction."

But for the time being, the only direction that Dinny was heading was towards Athlone. After Clara station, Mick Gavin retrieved the jar of porter that his fireman had hid. Both of them were half fluthered, but they reached Athlone all the same.

Mick lived in a little Westmeath village called Ballinahown. As the train came over Corracullin Bog, Dinny took over driving and let him jump out with his bicycle to cycle the few miles home. With a quick wave behind him, the driver cycled down a country lane and came out somewhere near the crossroads at Doon. He had planned to stay at home all day and catch the next train coming back.

Dinny could drive as well as he could stoke. After dropping Mick off he was able to keep the train going – over the railway bridge at the River Boor, past Fardrum and on to Athlone. He was as skilled as any fireman and because of that, he didn't have to keep stoking the engine all the time. Experience allowed him to finish the rest of the journey on his own. Without Mick, he could gauge the fire, making sure that it was low in front under the arch, and high at the sides and back. When he had things the way he wanted them, he could take a rest for himself.

CHAPTER TWENTY-NINE

Jam at Galls

One evening, as he was reading the newspaper, my father heard the distant sound of an engine and went to investigate. Outside, the moon had risen and the sky was full of stars. Overhead, a lone aeroplane droned south towards the Slieve Bloom Mountains. As he stood there, he lit his pipe and watched the bluish smoke as it trailed into the night air. Eventually he returned indoors and announced to us all:

"Well do you know what? They're bumming Dublin out of it!"

The war had been raging for a couple of years but if there was just one plane flying over, it seemed to my father that there were a hundred in the sky. There was trouble in Belfast, but he always worried that they would come and let them drop where we were. England was pretty bad and on one occasion there was a bombing in Dublin, which I remember well because it caused an awful fire down the North Strand and burned it out.

Each week, my mother was given a ration book registered with the shops in Clara and she kept it as part of the housekeeping. The consumer's name and address was written into it, and there were coupons for butter and other essential items.

During the Emergency, the Government asked the farmers in Offaly to produce more food, which they did so that we never went hungry for meat or vegetables. Orchards such as Clavin's and Johnston's supplied us with fruit, but we found other things harder to come by.

For instance, our sugar entitlement was just a few ounces per person. Fortunately, my father was very great with Sean Kelly of D.E. Williams in Clara, who always gave him loads because he was fond of putting a week's ration in his tea. On one occasion, he came home with an extra portion hidden in his coat, but it wasn't until he noticed the last few grains of sugar on his shoe that he realised there had been a hole in his pocket.

During the war years, there was only one train running each day, on account of the lack of coal available to the G.S.R. A few railway branches were even shut down, and the company was only saved from closing at one point by the release of government supplies. When I set out for Dublin one morning to spend the day with Joe's new wife, Rose, we were doing well since for some people going further – say to Cork – a journey by train could last a *whole* day!

That evening, we returned to Kingsbridge in good time for the only returning train, and Dinny saw us off from the station. By the time that the engine reached Portarlington however, the driver, who had been using nuggets of caked coal dust, could go no further, so all the passengers had to alight and make their own arrangements.

There we were, sitting stranded on a station bench with hardly any money between us. When we explained our predicament to one of the porters, he told us that there was a train going back to Dublin. I decided that we would have a better chance of getting accommodation there than we would traipsing around Portarlington, so I asked for permission to use the station telephone.

As our train pulled back into Kingsbridge, Dinny stood bemusedly on the platform.

"Where are ye going at all?" he laughed. "I said goodbye and now here ye are coming back again!"

Nevertheless, refusing to see us stuck, he took us over to his digs in Inchicore – a house on a hill with steep steps going up to it.

We stood shivering at the front door until the landlady answered.

"Would you oblige these two ladies by putting them up for tonight?" Dinny asked.

"You don't have to ask," she answered with a kind smile. "I wouldn't see you stuck."

Rose and I were lucky enough to get a bed between us for the night and a breakfast the next morning.

It brings to mind the yarn about the Yank who came to Ireland on holidays. Arriving at the station wearing a new boater hat, he spotted a porter standing against a wall with his cap turned sideways. "When is the next train due?" he asked. "Oh let me see now," the porter replied, and withdrew a shabby timetable from his pocket. "Well would you believe it!" he exclaimed shaking his head. "The next train has just gone!"

Cycling to visit Bab, the road out to Rahan was bog on either side for two or three miles. I never felt that on the bike and would have a mile done without thinking. On the way, I always passed the house of a man called Paddy Malone. He used to go out to the gate at a time when jam was rationed, and if he saw a woman going to Clara on a bike for messages, he'd say, "Come here I want ye." Leaning conspiratorially over the handlebars of the woman's bike, he would pass on the latest intelligence: "There's jam at Galls!" That referred to a little huxtery shop nearby. With a grateful nod, the woman would turn in the direction of Galls, knowing that she was only wasting time taking her empty jam jars into town.

By that time, Jack had got a house in the Derries and he brought up his family there. I was often there in time for the Rosary. "'Ah Bab," he used to plead. "Sure won't three Hail Marys do for tonight?"

"Come on now Jack," she would reply sternly. "We'll be only a few minutes." Then, putting his bare feet onto the warm turf stacked beside the fire, he would let his wife begin.

> '*Hail Mary, full of Grace…*'
> [*sound of motor*]
> "Lord, I wonder who that would be at this time of t'evening?"
> '*The Lord is with thee…*'
> "Jack, would you ever take a look out there?"
> '*Blessed art thou among women…*'
> "And see whether it's the priest or the doctor passing."
> '*Blessed is the fruit of thy womb, Jesus…*'
> [*a curtain is pulled across*]
> "Begod, it's the doctor right enough."

A deaf and dumb workman lived with them when they started the farm and he was a real saint. He worked in Clavins and then landed down with Bab, who used to feed him because he was doing odd jobs for her. For years, he was always to be found in the yard or working around the back, and he used to drive the family to Mass in the horse and trap. He couldn't talk and Bab could trust him to mind the children. They had him sleeping in an oul' outhouse, and he loved Bab and wouldn't leave her at all. No matter if he were in the far part of the Kingdom of Kerry, he'd walk to her.

Nanny Carroll also kept a workman because she lived by herself and he was handy to have about the place. His name was Heffernan, but he was known to all as 'Humpy Heffernan'. Like most workmen, he had been raised in an orphanage before being sent to the Union, and he felt so delighted and privileged to be free that Nanny was able to keep him for a fraction of the wages that are due now.

One day, Bab watched as the same hat-bedecked figure approached the house.

"There's oul' Nanny Carroll coming on for town," Bab cried.

"She'll bring the messages."

True to form, the old woman arrived into the yard, alighted from the crossbar and said, "The Lord save us. I couldn't go by without passing."

"Nanny, would you ever bring me a pound of butter?" Bab asked.

"Oh Lord, sure amn't I goin' that way," she replied.

When she returned a couple of hours later, she sat at the end of the table, adjusted her hat and handed the butter over. Then she counted out the change and put it on the table. She had been given a pound but after all the shuffling, she gave her back the change of a ten-shilling note.

"Wait now," Bab said. "I think there's a mistake here."

With that, the old woman shot out of the chair.

"Oh Jaysus Christ, Babby!" she exclaimed.

You'd swear that someone had stuck a knife in her.

"Hould on," Bab said softly, taking Nanny's big hand in her own. "Don't worry. Sure it's not the killing of a man."

CHAPTER THIRTY

The Cards are Dealt (1943)

One Saturday, a group of neighbours arrived out to Kilmucklin to play cards. Together with my father and my mother who were sitting at the end of the table, there was a group of nine. But when my mother won the rubber worth £10, she just quietly laid her cards down. In his excitement, my father took hold of her.

"God dammit!" he cried. "Wouldn't you think you'd get excited; throw it out and hit the table with it?'

If that were him, he'd hit the table and rise everything on it. I, on the other hand, could be very cagey. Once everyone else had shown their hand, I'd say, "Hold on there now. I've to play yet."

Since she had won all the money in the pot, my father put it down on her side of the table. Then she went on and decided to play another game. But when the cards had been dealt, she stood up suddenly.

"I'm not on the next round," she said. "I'm not playing."

She hobbled into the bedroom and the remaining players had to deal again.

Feeling a little concerned, I followed her into the room which was next to the road. The curtains were pulled over and when I opened the door, a stream of light from the kitchen fell across the bed. Still dressed, she sat up and blinked. When she saw who it was, she looked at me reproachfully.

"Will you go down?' she whispered hoarsely. "Your father'll be the next that'll be up."

But I was worried, so I sat on the bed beside her and took her

The Cards are Dealt (1943)

big hand in my own.

"Are you feeling alright Mam?" I asked.

"I'm going to bed because I have a pain," she admitted.

Deciding not to question her further, I helped her take her clothes, truss and apron off, and closed the door gently behind me.

Meanwhile, the card game in the kitchen was in full swing and went on until twelve o'clock. When the neighbours had gone, tea was made and everyone sat around. I couldn't sit still because I was very worried about my mother. When I went into the bedroom, I saw that she had turned over, so I shook her gently.

"Will you have a cup of tea, Mam?" I asked.

"Ah no," she replied drowsily. "Don't give me anything. I'm alright."

She seemed to be dozing off, and when my father came in, he looked at her anxiously.

"Are you alright?" he asked.

"I'm grand," she whispered. 'I'm going to go asleep."

After the cards had been put away, we went to bed. Later that night however, I woke with a feeling of dread. Hearing muffled voices in the next room, I pressed my ear to the wall.

"Ah," I heard my mother say, "you know I'm going to give you an advice. It's a very short life so never neglect your Mass and your confession."

She said that because my father was very heedless. The priest knew him well because he only went to confession every six months.

"Never miss your Mass," she persisted, "because you know it's very hard to get into Heaven."

"Arra, will you go out of that," my father replied. "What harm did you ever do?"

Then it turned to a discussion about Heaven and Hell until eventually my father turned over and went to sleep.

After some fitful dreams, I woke again and the moonlight was just enough to light the dial of my watch. It was half past two. I could still hear my mother moaning and it upset me.

'Jesus,' I said to myself. 'She has the pain still.'

I went out to her and oh Lord, she couldn't get her breath! In a panic, I ran in and shook Tommie.

"I don't think Mam is well," I cried.

With that my father, who was a heavy sleeper, jumped out of bed and yelled:

"Will you get some of the lads to go for the doctor immediately!"

Coming near morning, young Dr O'Hara arrived. He had just qualified and I had heard that he was an awful man for drink. Nevertheless, he was all we had at that unsociable hour, and my father was grateful to him. He was shown into the room where my mother was lying. Sitting on the side of the bed, he took her temperature, asked us how long she had been feeling sick, and took a needle from his leather bag.

There was an avenue down to the gate, so my father went down to be polite and to leave the doctor out to the road. While he was gone, I went in to see how my mother was feeling, but when I tried to prop her up in the bed, she fell on top of my arm. She was a big woman and I could hardly get my arm out. As I tried to free myself I could see her face changing as she slipped into unconsciousness.

One morning, just a few months earlier, she had been working contentedly in the kitchen. She went barefoot into the yard at the back of the house but as she was coming in, she stubbed her toe against the stone step. Naturally when I heard her hit the ground, I came running. On that occasion, I had been very worried until I heard a peal of laughter come from the pile of cloth prostrate on the floor. This time however, she was beyond laughter and just lay there as still as a sack of spuds.

But when my father came back into the bedroom, he tried for his wife's sake to be optimistic.

"Now," he said cheerfully. "The doctor's after getting you a prescription. Ned'll go down to Pettitt's for the bottle and you'll be grand."

But when she didn't answer, he saw through it. Putting his hand to his mouth, he fell silent and stood helplessly in the little room.

We decided then to send for Father McCormack. All the local people sought him out when somebody they knew was seriously ill, and many stories were told about him. Once while visiting the house of a woman who was close to death, he was greeted in the yard by a young lad who had been instructed to wait until the priest arrived.

"Hold that horse till I go into this sick call," he snapped. "If you don't hold it," he said, "I'll stick you to the ground."

'Ah, but Father," the boy replied, with childlike reasoning. "Wouldn't it be better to stick the horse?"

Towards evening, the same well-loved priest with his small round-framed glasses and portly face arrived on horseback, having come across the fields and ditches to get to our house. Patting my father on the shoulder, he was taken in his riding breeches and boots into the bedroom to see my mother. A deathly silence lay over the bed where she lay, and Father McCormack knelt down to give her the last rites.

The priest never told me, but both my father and I knew my mother was dying. She was unconscious and I don't know whether she could hear us, but after he had finished praying over her, Father McCormack went out to the gate to tell a neighbour the news.

"Poor Mrs Gaynor is going to Heaven," he said.

I sat by my mother's side and held her hand tightly as she began to fail. I was the last person with her in this world and as she breathed her last, I whispered the *Act of Contrition* into her ear:

> *Oh my God, I am heartily sorry for all my sins,*
> *And I firmly purpose by thy holy grace,*
> *Never more to offend thee,*
> *And to do all that I can,*
> *To atone for my sins,*
> *Amen.*

Numbly, I stood up from the bed and walked into the lads' room. Quietly I told them the news and when they were ready, we walked down to Saturday Mass together. There, we told many of our neighbours and the following night, the house was full of people.

My mother, who was seventy-two when she died, was waked at home because there was no such thing then as going to hospital or anything like that. She was laid out in a brown habit by two neighbouring women, who placed lighted candles near the bed and simple rosary beads between her joined hands. Having entered the world in lamp and candle-light, she went out of it the same way, without ever experiencing electricity or the conveniences it heralded. She had worked hard all her life to rear a big family and now we were all with her, looking after her.

All of Larry's pals were there and they came from everywhere. Dressed in a fine coat, Mrs White walked from the pub in Clara to Kilmucklin, and she was a big shot in our estimation. Perhaps she believed that my mother's standing as a Burke from Kilmucklin warranted such a long walk in the cold.

In those days, when you went to a wake, there was often a table with a basket on it, left out as a collection for the funeral Mass. Everybody you saw would put in a half crown which amounted to two and sixpence each. If the mourner was nearer to the family they might put in a pound. Some of those belonging to my father came down from Dublin where the tradition was dying out and, not realising that the money was to be given to the church, they thought it was all going to him. The parish priest got half of the money and the remainder was divided among the two curates.

There was a good bit of drink taken, and my father was after that because he nearly lost his mind. He was so deranged that you could give him all Guinness's and it wouldn't set him drunk. When one of the neighbours made a move to go after him out the back door, I grabbed his arm.

"Let him go," I said sadly. "He needs to be on his own for a while."

At the back of the house, Larry had built a shed where he carried on his carpentry work. There, my father stood amongst the ash stocks and half-planed felloes of unfinished cartwheels and wept for my mother. For forty-one years they had been so united as a couple and he couldn't accept the suddenness of her death. Ned took it bad but Larry was the worst. He had been working in Roscrea when he heard the news.

That Sunday evening, the remains were brought by two horses with black plumes to St Brigid's Church in Clara. The road behind was thronged with people walking into town to pay their respects. The subdued and black-garbed women, were joined by their husbands who wore diamond-shaped pieces of crepe, and together we marched past the drawn curtains of the town. For those still given to wry remarks, it was a case of 'stand into the funeral and let the forge pass by' – something the mixed-up hardware shop owner McGlynn had once said when out for an evening stroll.

My father had collected enough money by Monday to pay for High Mass. The service, which had five priests serving, cost £5 but he was anxious to spare no expense. The funeral was held in the afternoon and Ned and Tommie, wearing long Crombie coats, headed the coffin bearers. As I watched them bear the casket slowly through the gates of the Monastery Graveyard, I felt particularly sorry for poor Ned. That morning, as he sat at the fire, he had let out a great shout, crying, "I hope that I never did anything to annoy her!"

It was a dry winter's day and there were people there from the highest to the lowest, and during her life she had shown great charity to them all.

My mother was buried near the top of the graveyard, near the stone castellated wall that cut off the cemetery from the main road. As the sods of earth hit the polished wood with a dull thud, we turned our faces away from the coffin and began to huddle into small groups, quietly discussing events amongst each other.

"She was great while she was in it," Frank Clyne said, touching my shoulder.

Turning to face him, I gazed into the face of a lonely, tired-looking man. Although I had to search hard to find a trace of the young butcher I had once known, I mustered up some encouraging words of my own.

"Arra, you're very good to your own mother, Frank," I replied. "May God be good to her."

Meanwhile, my father was having a harder time of it. As we filed out of the cemetery, a local man caught up with him at the iron turnstile.

"Ah, sure Tom," he said, "aren't you grand, haven't you Kathleen?"

My father turned to him bitterly, and looked him in the eye.

"Jaysus," he spat. "How long am I going to have her?"

After we returned from the funeral, the house was full of neighbours, but after a while, they trickled home in ones and twos until eventually only old Tom Doorley was left. Eventually even he made for the door.

"I'll hit the road a welt," he said loudly, standing to fix the cap on his head.

After Tom had gone out by the 'presbytery,' a small, subdued group was left around the hearth. Our cousin Jody Spollen from Daingean sat beside Larry and next to him were four of the Robbinses. We all sat talking about my mother and about the way that she went. While we chatted, we could hear an awful lot of crickets chirping like little birds in the chimney.

Addressing nobody in particular, Jody who was gazing at the flames suddenly said, "You won't hear them any more." That was supposed to be a sign because my mother had died.

Sure enough, there were no crickets, but I don't think it was down to anything that Jody Spollen believed. That was just *piseróg* out and out. While the crickets *crkk-crkk*ed away, Ciss went to the range, boiled a big kettle of water and scalded the heart and lungs out of them.

None of us slept very well after the day of the funeral. Instead we took small naps whenever our grief would allow us. One night, after lying in bed for some time, I eventually dozed off. When I awoke, everything was quiet in the room. Suddenly, my mother appeared standing at the door, holding a little eggcup full of whiskey because I had gone to bed with woman's pain. I could always tell her about the little aches and pains I had. When I realised she was dead, I let out a roar and the next thing I remembered were my brothers all over me, pulling and dragging to calm me down.

After that, they got a girl that was very great with us called Kathleen Fox to come up to the house. They wouldn't let me sleep alone anymore because they didn't know what would happen to me. I might have a dream of her.

I missed my mother so much that I had a vision of her standing at the door. Being around her and loving her so much with everyone codding her, it was hard to believe that she was gone, but in the end it was my father who suffered the most.

The eleventh came and went and we still had to plan for Christmas. That December was unusually prosperous for Clara, considering the state of affairs with the war. A large amount of money arrived from Clara people working in England to those at home, and the jute mills had been working full time for some weeks. People everywhere were showing signs of festivity, and both the Clara Fife and Drum Band and the Pipe Band were rehearsing for Christmas morning.

Our house was packed to the roof with people, big lumps of ham hanging up everywhere and my father was like a madman in the middle of it all. Soon after, my mother's war ration book was sent back, marked 'dead' on the front cover to the Department of Supplies in Dublin. My father almost lost his cool, because he had thought he was going to have his wife forever and in the end she went out like a match in the middle of all the preparations.

Like him, we couldn't feel any of the enjoyment that we should have been feeling, but we tried to celebrate Christmas the best way we could. On Stephen's Day I went into the parlour room. The big, framed picture of my mother was still hanging there and I gazed up at it sadly.

"For the love of God, look at him," I implored. "Will you do something for him?"

My mother's eyes gazed silently out of the photograph as if to say that she would do her best.

"You're not here now," I whispered. "When this is all over, there'll be just me."

She was surely looking down from Heaven praying for me, because I had lived with her day in and day out, and when God took her I was lost.

CHAPTER THIRTY-ONE

Visit to Kilminchy

Dinny and his sister Kate were waiting for me at Maryborough station when I arrived. Alighting from the carriage, I hugged him warmly and shook Kate's hand. A spinster in her fifties, she wore heavy lisle stockings and had her hair in a bun, with small round-framed glasses to match. Her few remaining teeth were quite noticeable when she smiled.

"How are ye Kathleen Gaynor?" she lilted.

I was there on account of a letter I had received from Dinny. In the New Year, his bedridden mother had died, so he wrote and asked me to come to visit. I had often relied on my own mother, especially when it came to keeping my father in the dark, and I still didn't want him finding out where I was.

Nevertheless, I had stuck to my plans and now we were clipping out to Kilminchy in a donkey and cart. A much more obliging animal than our pony, the donkey was fitted with a harness improvised from an old corset. After passing the prison on our left, it plodded up a long straight hill.

"One of these days, we might go out as far as the Rock of Dunamaise, if it's fine," Dinny enthused over the sound of the rolling wheels. "And if you play your cards right, we'll get down to Bannon's Dancehall."

According to tradition, there ought not to be any diversion of any kind for at least six months after a family death, but I didn't think of that.

"I'll have the head of the hen so." I was quite heedless when it came to tradition.

Soon, we reached the top of the road and veered right until a thatched house sitting in a hollow off the main road came into view. It had whitewashed mud walls and flower-filled window boxes along each sill. There was a pond to the right with ducks and geese, and parsnips and carrots grew at the back.

Dinny helped me to carry my suitcase through the high gate – also improvised through the use of springs from an old corset – down the path and past a small orchard. The ground underneath was littered with apples going brown and as we stepped over these, the half door beckoned, inviting us into a stone-floored kitchen. The land in front of the house was lower than the kitchen, because it was from there that the yellow clay needed to build it had been dug. When Kate made jelly, she always covered it in muslin and left it to set in one of the deep window recesses, which never took long because the walls had been built thick. It made for a natural fridge in the heat of summer.

Once my eyes adjusted to the darker light of the kitchen, I could see that against the back wall stood a dresser with a rack of old-fashioned delph, along the top of which was arranged an assortment of well-polished kettle and pot lids. Most of the plates were cracked or in half, but through careful arrangement of each piece, one behind the other, Kate gave the impression that she had enough crockery to supply a hotel. To the right was a large fireplace upon which a crane hung. To the left of the fireplace, sugar and other luxuries were kept dry in a cupboard.

The whole room smelled of onions or 'inyins' as Kate called them. A rolling pin lay on a table coated with flour, where she had been making some bread for my visit. There were two bedrooms – one on each side of the kitchen and Dinny had a room to himself. Up around the field at the back was a pig shed and a fairy tree that nobody would touch. The tree, which was an old hawthorn, stood about fifty yards behind the house. Even when Dinny's father, William Houlihan was alive and working as a farm labourer, he would not go near it for fear of the fairies.

That evening, we sat down to a lovely tea. Kate beamed toothlessly across the table at Dinny.

"Begod, Dinny Houlihan, but you're a real Government Man," she enthused, cutting the brown bread into nice, even slices. "Your brothers could do something to take a leaf out of your book. Peter Houlihan is working above in Rathbrennan chopping up oul' turnips for cows," she said, casting a disparaging glance at Dinny's younger brother, who she constantly scolded.

"But you're kept busy all the same," I ventured; taking note of Peter's friendly, open countenance.

Haughtily, Kate retrieved a steaming potato from the bowl in the centre of the table.

"The divil of busy he is, and he 'atin' plates of pahehs and making a rum pum pooslum of the place," came her dismissive reply.

"Oh begod aye, Rathbrennan," said Peter, ignoring his sister's last remark. "An' t'oul' feed salesman come up from Waterford and started telling Johnny Higgs all about how the turnips is nothing only eigthy per cent waher, but I had the answer for him."

We waited for Peter to butter a slice of bread and then tell us what the witty response might have been.

"Well if eighty per cent is waher," he said between mouthfuls, "what's d'other hundred per cent made from?"

Since Mrs Houlihan had died, Kate was responsible for the running of the house. She constantly scolded her two brothers, Jim and Peter, but Joe, who was almost a man of the roads, always stayed out of her way.

She was always cleaning, but then spoiled it by talking too much. After she had finished inside, she was in the habit of looking at the house from the road. If everything was as it should be, she went out on to remove rubbish from the verges.

On one occasion, Jimmy Higgs went to help the owner of one of the few rare cars in those days to find a hubcap that had fallen onto the road. The driver was sure he had lost it in the vicinity of Kilminchy pump, so the two men went to check there. Unfortunately, despite their best efforts, they were eventually forced to concede defeat. About a year later however, while Jimmy was attempting to fix Kate's broken bed frame, he looked up and found to his surprise that hanging on the wall was a Sacred Heart picture framed perfectly by the erstwhile hubcap.

While she was scouring the roadside for such 'ornaments', Kate also came across groups of hikers, which she called 'pikers'. There might be four or five lads together, and they often came as far as the door to take photographs or to ask for a drink of water.

To supplement her small pension of nine shillings while she was alive, Dinny's mother had the field at the back let to the Whelan family for £15. That guaranteed the family some sort of income for the year. There was a pig kept in a pen at the back of the house and the Whelans, who also farmed a field at the back of a neighbouring family called Fleming, supplied it with turnips.

One afternoon Arthur Whelan, Jimmy Graham and young O'Meara were working hard when lunch-time came. Soon, Kate came across with tea and sandwiches. The teapot, which was an old-fashioned implement, had a strangely shaped spout, but while she poured the tea, no comment was made.

After she had returned to the house, Jimmy Graham made comment

"Arthur," he asked, "what sort of a teapot do you suppose that was?"

"Well Jimmy," Arthur replied, the pot reminding him of something that people normally kept under beds. "That's an oul' chamber pot that Kate uses to piss in!"

But the main talking point when I arrived was that Kate was doing a strong line with Paddy Hannon from Ballylynan. Early on, he had insisted on finishing with her, on account of the Houlihans not having 'the electric', but then Kate went and found some broken light bulbs and strung them up with string.

On my last evening, Paddy arrived by bicycle. When Kate announced that they were on their way into Mar'borough, her two brothers breathed a sigh of relief. Peter waited until she had closed the gate and then made a sign from the garden to let him know she had gone. Jim came away from the little window and said to me, "Now I'll whistle a tune and you dance." He shut the half door against the evening air and with the fire lighting, the plates and kettle-lids on the dresser shone like new. When Dinny came out to sit by the hearth, he was delighted to see me dancing to the hornpipe that his brother was whistling. After a little while, there was a lull in the music and we had tea.

"Well I'm away so," Jim said then, patting his knees and standing up from the fire. "I'm goin' down to the pump."

"Mind yourself," Dinny replied. Outside, he unstabled the donkey and harnessed it to a water barrel that ran on two wheels, one of which was noticeably bigger than the other. This difference caused the animal to list to the side, but he managed somehow and was soon on his way.

Once man and donkey had creaked away on their uneven wheels, the silence was restored, save for the spit and hiss of new wood on the hearth.

"You know, sometimes I think we should get away too," I murmured.

"To the pump?" asked Dinny.

"Well not exactly," I said. "It's just that when my poor mother was alive, I could always tell her I'd a date on, but sometimes my father would find out, and he'd tell her she was only making a stick to beat herself with. Then the two of us had to be more secret."

"So what's the difference now?" Dinny said, pausing to look up the chimney at the few ragged stars that had appeared in the evening sky.

"Well you know what I mean. Even though I was the victim, I had her at my back. Now I know I'm going to get the works from my father."

"Arra, don't be worrying now about what he thinks," Dinny said, raking the hearth. "Sure maybe we'll get a place above in Dublin."

When Jim returned with the water, he was eager for more dancing, so we whiled away another hour. Eventually we heard the gate swinging open and the sound of footsteps coming up the path.

Although we all waited for Kate and her boyfriend to come through the half-door, we hung on in vain. Their voices rang out along the gable wall, causing Jim to remark that they must be on their way to the 'motor' – a hay-filled, rust-covered vehicle that had been lying at the end of the field for about twenty years. The fact that it had a thatched roof didn't bother Kate and her boyfriend because they had no intention of driving anywhere.

When Kate eventually came in on the half door and hung her coat on the hook, Jim eyed her sullenly from his seat at the fire. As we made tea, his demeanour grew even sourer. Finally, as she took out her hairpin to comb her hair for bed, she noticed him sulking.

"What's wrong with you?" she asked.

"What's wrong with me?" Jim cried incredulously. "You should be ashamed of yourself, carrying on like that. I'll burn that car because…because…it's nothing but a den of sin!"

CHAPTER THIRTY-TWO

Night before the Wedding

"Boys, ye're in the right place," my father said, sitting heavily on a bar-stool beside the railway Inspector.

He removed his hat and wiped his rain-soaked forehead with a grey handkerchief. The men had a round in so my father tossed his few pence across the counter and let the stout settle in his own glass.

It was Monday night and Stephen Fitz had taken Lar and I into Clara in his taxi, so that we could make a night of it before the wedding. Three years had now passed since my mother's death and I had been faced with making some tough decisions. Although nobody realised it, that morning I had almost decided not to get married.

At Kilcoursey, I had sat and explained my predicament to Father McCormack: "I don't know whether I'll get married at all or not because my father is kicking up."

The priest was sympathetic.

"Don't mind your father," he said. "You've a young life before you and he'll never give in, because he's out for his own comfort, the same as any man."

"God, I think you're right, Father."

"Go ahead,' he concluded, showing me to the door. "I'll have you married early in the morning."

My father meanwhile, shunning any offer of company, had driven despite the rain, into White's in the pony and trap. There he joined the men, including the florid-faced railway Inspector,

Dinny Byrne, who was the best man and a friend of Dinny's from Harold's Cross.

The men were in high spirits and Dinny, who sat enjoying his last night as a bachelor, knew the pub well. On many occasions, he had run down there for a half measure while his engine was taking on water at the station.

While he waited, my father removed a crumpled newspaper from a coat pocket. With a disapproving eye, he noticed that the top of the front page was still mottled with blots of water where it had taken the brunt of the February shower. Barely glancing at Dinny, he took it over to the fire and toasted it over the flames for a minute, taking care not to let the pages burn. As he fanned the wet paper, an occasional spark spat onto the hot flagstone.

Awkwardly, Dinny approached him.

"Your pint is there waiting for you, Mr Gaynor," he enthused. "Are you not going to join us?"

The old man turned to face him.

"None of that matters a damn. Now listen, you needn't tell me anything. You stole my sunshine, and if you're going to say something – don't bother."

With a shrug, he turned back towards the fire.

Now I don't think that he knew what he was saying, because he was already as drunk as an owl. Unhappy, and having fallen out of company with the other men, he aimed to drink faster than they did. His nose was a bit out of joint, and now it was running through his head that there would be no one to get him a bit to eat or anything. He had nothing against Dinny, but he was selfish as a man.

Later that night, I joined Larry and D.E. Williams' staff Sean Kelly, Mairead and Eileen O'Halloran in the snug of White's. By now, the girls were close friends of mine and usually came out to Kilmucklin every Wednesday for tea. For these visits, I carved up an apple tart or scones I had made and chatted about my plans. Kelly, who sat with us, still enjoyed his lunchtime drink and once had to be carried when he fell at a party of Ciss's in Dun Laoghaire. Despite this, he was good company and the hours passed quickly. After a little while, we remembered that we were all up early the following morning. Since the weather was bad, we agreed to call it a night.

There had been no let up at all during the time we were in White's and the roads and neighbouring fields had become more and more waterlogged. By late evening, the Brosna had risen to a great height and in some places, flocks of gulls floated on the floodwater.

In the semi-darkness of White's yard, my father stood in the rain and pulled roughly at the pony's harness. Then, reaching for the whip, he strode alongside the trap and climbed up. As I ascended the metal step, my feet slid in the greasy wet and I drew the blanket around my head in an effort to keep dry, counting the seconds until Larry climbed in beside me.

Soon after leaving Main Street, I noticed that my father's foul mood had been worsened by drink. Overtaking council workers who were too busy pumping water to notice us, we passed the sandbag-choked doorways of River Street and came out under the railway bridge.

Suddenly, we turned down a narrow country lane and ran into a flood that almost reached the shafts of the trap. By now, the rain had stopped and the moon appeared from behind a cloud, reflecting off the dark water and frightening the pony. Being on the beer, my father couldn't see the danger and started to hit the poor animal with the whip.

All he got in return was a snort of steam and a sideways shake of the pony's wet mane. Knowing nothing about weddings or the hundred other things that bothered humans, it lumbered on regardless, drawing sheets of water sideward in its wake.

I wished that I could be just as heedless, but all that I could think about was that whoever came up with the idea for the trap gave it a right name, since we might all be caught if it turned over.

Larry put a hand out to the door and whispered to me, "You jump out if he keeps using the whip like that."

He knew that we might flounder into a submerged dike. At the very least, the wheels were getting a great swelling from being driven through the flood water, and the metal rims creaked and tightened awfully.

As we came up the hill, our pace slowed but my father lashed the animal's flanks with the whip and called it every name he could think of. Larry was concerned for my safety and made a drive at my father to grab the reins off him until, with flaring nostrils and rolling eyes, the pony began to labour nervously under the tugging it was getting.

'Oh Sacred Heart of Jesus,' I whispered, 'I place all my trust in Thee.'

When, rain-soaked and sullen, we eventually passed between the flooded gate posts of Kilmucklin, I thanked the man above.

****

I awoke with a start when the alarm clock rang at six o'clock. Outside the house, you couldn't see the sides of the road for the water and all around the gate was the very same as an ocean. I hadn't got a wedding dress: I dressed myself quite plainly instead with a lovely coat and shoes. My ring had been handed down to me by my mother a few years before, and I had new gold put around it where it had become worn.

In the kitchen, there was little in the way of decent conversation, since my father had no intention of coming to the church.

Attempting to boil the kettle, he just sat at the hearth and fanned the flames with his hat. I left him to it because I had too much to think about. Then, after packing my suitcase, a thought struck me that I should look for something of my mother's to take with me to Dublin. After all, my father hadn't given me anything in the way of a dowry. Slipping into the parlour room, I went to the sideboard and ran my hand over the little ornaments until my eye settled on the porcelain figures of a little cavalier and his lady. I wrapped them carefully in paper and put them at the bottom of my case.

When everything was packed, I walked out the door without a word to my father and met Stephen Fitz, who was ready to take me to the church. It was a big gesture on his part. With fuel still rationed after the war, God only knows how he came by the petrol. Elsewhere across the country, cars were gathering rust in garages and yards, but the taxi driver never gave it a second thought.

"God, you're shocking hard on me,'" yawned Father McCormack as he started the ceremony.

He had agreed to marry us at seven o'clock because the Dublin train was leaving at nine. Besides Dinny Byrne who was brought down as Dinny's best man, I had my cousin Minny Burke as my bridesmaid. That was a concession to my father who didn't show up in the end. There was no one else but the four of us, a couple of friends and Father McCormack in the empty church. Afterwards, having had to fast from midnight the night before, we set off eagerly across the Fair Green to Joe's house for the wedding breakfast.

"Lord, Father, I think I'll get married myself," Larry said as he sat down. Before replying, the priest wiped his mouth carefully with a handkerchief.

"Look at poor Joe, for all the good it done him," he replied simply, gesturing towards the room where Nancy Sullivan lay.

And as for me – well you'd swear that there was something wrong with me. In those days, every wedding merited a small piece in the *Independent*, but we were never mentioned. People in Clara said, "Oh poor Kathleen, she's gone. Sure she had to be married." They thought that the wedding was a sudden affair on account of me becoming pregnant, but in reality I was about six months married before I conceived.

Larry had promised that he wouldn't go to England while my mother was alive, because that would break her heart. When she died however, it was a dead house and he swore that he wouldn't be long after me. After I had gone, he strode through the floodwaters on a pair of homemade stilts and climbed a hill to look down on Kilmucklin.

"In the name of Christ," he sighed. "What am I going to do now?"

CHAPTER THIRTY-TWO

Bringing Bread to Make Peace

In those days, the tradition was that you didn't go home until you were nearly a month married, so I waited until one morning in March. My first stop was D.E. Williams', and when the bell rang above the door, Mairead who was relieving for Miss O'Halloran came out to see who it was. Her eyes widened in delight. 'Cat!' she screamed and threw her arms around me.

Later, as we sat drinking tea, she shook her head and laughed.

"Did you not realise what you done sending that postcard?" she said. "Just think about it for a minute and it'll come to you."

Obliging her, I thought about the card, which had been intended to say something about Miss O'Halloran's crush over Tommie. I had eventually found one that read something like, 'I'm in love but aren't I almost bald?' I was delighted because she was sure to laugh about the idea of being in love.

"Well, begod anyhow," Mairead continued, sipping her tea. "Didn't Peter Flattery fire the letters in one morning and your card was in the bundle. O'Halloran never put her hand on it because I was quick enough to tear it up before she got back."

"What did you do that for?" I quipped, slightly annoyed until suddenly it dawned on me. Miss O'Halloran was going bald! With renewed feelings of gratitude towards Mairead for keeping my friendship with Miss O'Halloran intact, I continued on my way to Kilmucklin.

When I arrived, my father shed tears of joy because he couldn't believe it. At that time of the day Tommie was working, so he was on his own trying to kindle the fire and boil the kettle with his hat and coat on. I noticed that he had milked the three cows but left the pails where the dog could drink from them. They were such bad housekeepers that it was obvious there was no woman in it.

"Jesus," I muttered. "What'll become of you at all?"

"Well the house could har'ly look after itself," my father snapped. Dismissively, I rolled up my sleeves like a burly midwife.

"The come-outs of you and you still sitting with nothing done," I said. "Stand out there 'til I regulate things. At least I can get you a cup of tae itself."

I soon set about putting the house to rights, and when Larry arrived home from England a few days later, there were apple tarts cooling on the window-sill once more.

One evening, as the both of us sat in the parlour room, our conversation was disturbed by the muffled tones of Tommie's voice in the kitchen, so we put our ears to the door to listen.

"Father," Tommie said stoutly, "I want to tell you something." My father looked up from the paper in surprise, wondering what this announcement was going to be. "Now before you say anything," he continued, "I'm doing this for your sake. I'm going to get married."

There was a rustle of paper as the *Independent* hit the hearth.

"Jaysus," my father cried. "By all means get married, but don't do it for my sake!"

Then, hearing our tittering, he strode over to the parlour room door and flung it open.

"Come outside here," he ordered.

The game was up then, so I had nothing to lose from throwing my own spake in. Besides, a woman was what the house badly needed.

"Now," I said, with my hands on my hips. "While I'm here, let the girl come to visit."

On the day that Mary Purcell arrived out to Kilmucklin, anyone could see that she was certainly capable. Her father had died when she was only seven, leaving behind the big farm I had visited with Dinny. Her sister Stacia – the owner of half of Kilree Street in Bagenalstown – had fallen for Ned, and he said jokingly that he had to marry her soon, before she went out of her mind altogether.

Without doubt, Mary also had the makings of a thrifty and dependable wife for Tommie. When I boarded the train to return to Dublin, I was happier in myself. These thoughts did not come without a tinge of sadness however. I had perhaps asked too much of my father, and the hurt that I had caused him by leaving remained.

Nevertheless, as I sat in the carriage, I smiled to myself. Although I had fallen out with him over the wedding, I never wanted to see him on his own, and I knew that Tommie and Mary would bring some life back to Kilmucklin. My mother was looking down on them all.

And as for myself, I was reminded of the lines of a verse that my father had often himself quoted:

Any good that you can do, do it now.
Do not defer it, for you may not pass this way again.

EPILOGUE

As I came out of St Michael's Church one autumn day, I was surprised to see a familiar figure leaving Johnson, Mooney & O'Brien's with two big bags of cakes and bread. With mixed feelings of excitement and apprehension, I crossed the road to meet my father.

"Where are you going," I exclaimed, "with all of that and nobody here but Dinny and I?"

"Well I got you buns and I got you cakes and everything that was in it," he said, delighted to see me.

I looked him up and down. "Well come on so, and bring t'ass."

Anyone would think I had a hundred children, and I was sure I had enough to feed Mrs Walsh's family for a week.

When we arrived in Kingsbridge that February, we had nowhere to stay. In those days, you had to have three children to get a Corporation house, so we walked around Inchicore until we finally found a room to rent for ten shillings a week above a shop in Goldenbridge Gardens. Mrs Walsh lived upstairs and her husband knew Dinny well, because he worked in the railway shops.

When he came home at half five, Dinny was in the habit of hoisting his bicycle onto his shoulder and carrying it up the flight of stairs to our room. Opening the door on this particular evening, he was surprised to see a visitor sitting at the table.

"More power," he said cheerfully and shook my father's hand.

"He's after bringing us loads of bread," I said as he hung up his coat behind the door.

"Begod, that's great," Dinny replied mildly.

The room itself was presentable. Our bed took up one part of it. I had hung lush curtains on the windows that Jerry Houlihan sent over from America, and there wasn't much furniture to speak of besides an old table. Dinny had made it himself, so I put a white tablecloth over it to hide the legs.

With hardly any brown flour to be had since the bad harvest, we enjoyed sitting down that evening to a tea of bakery bread and some duck eggs that Kate had brought.

I realised that I had missed my father, and I was sure that he felt the same way, but the few short years since my mother's death had aged him. He had always been a 'Hail fellow, well met,' kind of man, but now he seemed defeated somehow, as if some of the joy of living had died with her.

"How are you going on, work wise?" he asked Dinny. "Tommie says he doesn't see you on any of the ingins this weather."

"Well I'm doing mixed middlin', I suppose," Dinny joked nervously.

"As a matter of fact," I cut in, "Dinny is after giving up working as a fireman. Mr Walsh is after helping him to get work in the shops in Inchicore."

Taking a slow sip from his cup of tea, my father drank in this news carefully.

"Would you not have tried again for the driving?"

"Well the boss called me into t'oul' office and says, 'I know that you gave up the smoking, but I think you'd make a master driver and I want you to go for the exam. Look,' he says, 'the test part of it is just a formality. You know your engines and I'll make sure you have no problem getting the job.'"

"But Dinny has a nice job working in Inchicore," I explained, "and he's off every day at half five."

Surely my father had to understand that for Dinny to go back on the trains would mean leaving me, to stay overnight in places like Sligo or Athlone.

Afterwards, when Dinny had gone downstairs for milk, he chewed thoughtfully on a crust of bread.

"You'll be visiting Bab this year for your turkey," he said. "And you can pick up one for Ciss as well."

"I'd be glad of it," I replied. "I'm trying to watch what money we have."

"Well, no matter what minding you're doing, always make sure and leave your husband with plenty of money," he advised.

That meant that I was to keep Dinny with enough money for drink, but we weren't like that at all as a couple. It was just that my father was a different type of man altogether, and my heart was broken to look at him. I quickly changed the subject.

"So what made you bring all the bread?"

"Well," the old man replied, taking my two hands in his. "You only pass through this oul' world once."

He smiled briefly and then paused to listen.

In the distance, the sound of a goods engine shunting wagons came through the open window, before giving way to the rattle of children's voices clamouring in the street below.

My father stood up and strode over to the window. There was still plenty of time before the Rosary, but he might forego it now that his wife was no longer alive to remind him. For both of us, new possibilities were opening. I made tea for the second time and we waited for the messages.

"Well ye'll never believe it," Dinny cried when he finally returned, his face a picture of bewilderment. Resting the milk down on the table, he sat down and laughed heartily. "I was in the shop down below when an oul' wan come in asking for a *turnover*. I never heard tell of it. I stood there with Walsh – the both of us wonderin' which end of her to take first. 'Mebbe we could make a right job of it if I took her by the legs,' he says. Well she wasn't long about telling us it was bread she was after. Begod, we have an awful lot to learn about Dublin!"